A History *of the* World
in Seven Themes

A History of the World in Seven Themes

VOLUME TWO: SINCE 1400

Stewart Gordon

New York   Oxford

OXFORD UNIVERSITY PRESS

Oxford University Press is a department of the University of Oxford.
It furthers the University's objective of excellence in research, scholarship,
and education by publishing worldwide. Oxford is a registered trademark of
Oxford University Press in the UK and certain other countries.

Published in the United States of America by Oxford University Press
198 Madison Avenue, New York, NY 10016, United States of America.

For titles covered by Section 112 of the US Higher Education
Opportunity Act, please visit www.oup.com/us/he for the latest
information about pricing and alternate formats.

Library of Congress Cataloging-in-Publication Data

Names: Gordon, Stewart, 1945- author.
Title: A history of the world in seven themes / Stewart Gordon.
Description: New York; Oxford: Oxford University Press, [2022-] |
  Includes bibliographical references and index. | Contents: v. 1. Volume
  one. To 1600—v. 2. Volume two. Since 1400 | Summary: "A higher
  education history book for World History courses"—Provided by
  publisher.
Identifiers: LCCN 2021018800 (print) | LCCN 2021018801 (ebook) | ISBN
  9780190642440 (v. 1; paperback) | ISBN 9780190642457 (v. 2; paperback)
  | ISBN 9780190642488 (v. 1; epub) | ISBN 9780190642495 (v. 2; epub)
Subjects: LCSH: World history—Textbooks. | History—Study and teaching
  (Higher)
Classification: LCC D21 .G717 2022 (print) | LCC D21 (ebook) | DDC
  909—dc23
LC record available at https://lccn.loc.gov/2021018800
LC ebook record available at https://lccn.loc.gov/2021018801

Printing number: 9 8 7 6 5 4 3 2 1
Printed by LSC Communications, Inc.,
United States of America

Brief Contents

Contents

List of Maps

Preface

Some years ago I came across the Persian term *sar-o-pa* ("from head to foot") in two-hundred-year-old documents from western India. More research established that *sar-o-pa* was a ceremony at which a ruler (or someone noble) gave to a person he wanted to honor new and elegant robes, which usually included a shirt, pants, turban, waist-wrap, and shoes. By accepting the robes, the honoree was obligated to serve the ruler. Subsequent investigations and discussions with colleagues confirmed that rulers practiced this ceremony throughout Asia and North Africa, from China to Morocco, though each colleague had previously thought it a local custom.

This is why we study world history: to discern common rituals, problems, and patterns that do not stop at a territorial boundary. A history that accurately reflects the past must recognize that wars, battles, and empires (the stuff of more traditional histories) barely touch how lives were lived, whether as an artisan, slave, trader, soldier, pilgrim, or doctor. The discovery of the widespread nature of the ceremony of *sar-o-pa* suggests that we examine evidence from a global perspective and that the evidence include not just traditional written sources but nonwritten sources as well. World history is not about merely analyzing documents and amassing or memorizing facts. It is about learning to consider big questions that matter across the whole of human experience. Such themes do not stay in the past. They are the very stuff of our present and make us aware of our responsibilities to the future. In *A History of the World in Seven Themes* I invite students and teachers to analyze, debate, and consider a broad range of questions. I have benefitted in my understanding of the world from wrestling with these themes, and I believe that you will, too.

Written from a global perspective and grounded in recent scholarship, *A History of the World in Seven Themes* presents a substantially new approach to teaching, learning, and understanding world history.

First, the narrative focuses on *seven problems* that every society—historical or contemporary—must face, regardless of religion, political structure, ethnicity, language, or geographical location. All peoples at all times have grappled with food, loyalty, slavery, gender, pilgrimage, trade, and technology. By showing the different and similar ways in which societies have handled these fundamental issues, the book underscores the commonalities and diversity of human experience.

Second, each chapter features a different way of understanding the past. Historians typically rely on written documents, such as memoirs, government reports, and letters. When these sources are scarce historians turn to other disciplines for understanding the past: anthropology, archaeology, ecology, geography, art history, sociology, and economics. When there are no documents, understanding the past is still possible through the methods of science, such as DNA analysis, dendrochronology, microscopic material examination, analysis of trace elements, and microphotography of human bones. Chapters also focus on new historical researchers and the insightful questions they raise, modeling for students the process of historical inquiry and showing them that history is not simply something one reads about but something one *does*.

Third, the book presents the seven broad societal problems through the experiences of *guides*—that is, actual historical figures who were deeply affected by the chapter's theme. In almost all chapters the guide wrote a memoir or letters, which allows him or her speak to us directly from the past.

Fourth, each chapter opens with "The Big Picture," a section that connects the theme's context across broad historical periods and brings the theme into wide geographic regions. "The Bigger Picture" ends the chapter with the important implications and questions of the theme for our world today.

Although *A History of the World in Seven Themes* takes a thematic and narrative approach, chronology is not abandoned. Timelines in each chapter organize key events in the flow of history. The book, however, downplays "ages," such as the Neolithic Revolution, the Iron Age, and the Axial Age in favor of common problems, connections across broad swaths of the world, and connections to the present.

Chapter Topics

Chapter 1 foregrounds one of the oldest and most important themes of human history, a society's definition of gender. Gender is the social construction that defines people as male or female based on biological differences. There have always been people who could not or would not accept these labels. The chapter examines sex, sexuality, and gender in locations across the globe. Our guides are a Japanese poet, the founder of the Mughal dynasty in India, a European Renaissance nun, and a Canadian tribal elder.

Chapter 2 examines the problem of nationalism. Nationalism seeks to place loyalty to the nation above all other loyalties, such as allegiance to family, city, language, and ethnicity. The chapter focuses on Kenya, where nationalism struggled with colonialism. Our guide is Jomo Kenyatta, an African nationalist who explored nation building in England and Russia before returning home to lead Kenya's struggle for independence from Great Britain and then to serve as Kenya's first prime minister and later its first president.

Chapter 3 considers what technology is and how it works. We follow glass-making technology from its early importance in lenses through the changes that produced large plate-glass windows and skyscrapers. The chapter puts the problems and possibilities of technology in a broad context, asking whether or not technology was a "driver" of history. Our guides are Antony van Leeuwenhoek, an eighteenth-century Dutch businessman and scientist, and Albert Noe, who worked as a skilled craftsman in a glass factory in West Virginia in the first half of the twentieth century.

Chapter 4 takes up migration, examining both the long history of mass human movement and the current problems of economic and political migrants. Our three guides experienced migration to the United States very differently. One was an illegal migrant from Mexico; one married a US citizen from her own country of Iraq; and one was the wife of a fellow Ugandan, both granted refugee status.

Chapter 5 considers slavery as a ubiquitous feature of the ancient and the modern world. None of the philosophers or seers of the ancient world condemned slavery—not Confucius, Buddha, Muhammad, Jesus, or Socrates. Kings promulgated laws about slavery, attempting to clarify such messy issues as inheritance by the child of a master and a slave. The chapter considers who benefited from slavery. Our guide is a slave in Spanish Cuba, who lived through the struggles for independence, the period of American control, and the Cuban Revolution (1953–1959), which brought communist leader Fidel Castro to power.

Chapter 6 considers human rights as one of the most important themes of the modern world. The focus is on the discussion in the years after World War II (1937–1945) that led to the United Nations' adoption of the Universal Declaration of Human Rights. Our guide is American activist and First Lady Eleanor Roosevelt, who was chair of the drafting committee and put her stamp on the concerns and wording of the document.

Chapter 7 examines the environment, with a concentration on how European colonial conquests affected and continue to affect the economies of former colonial countries. The chapter looks in detail at tin mining in Malaysia and cotton cultivation in India as typical colonial extractive industries. Our guide is Tomé Pires, a Portuguese apothecary who spent the years 1512 to 1515 in Malacca, in southwestern Malaysia, immediately after the Portuguese conquest.

Acknowledgments

I wish to thank the following institutions, whose faculties invited me to speak on topics central to these two volumes: Asiatic Society of Mumbai, Pune University, Deccan College, Ambedkar University, and Garware College. Special thanks to Dr. N. D. Parekar and Dr. A. R. Patil of the History Department, Shivaji University, Kolhapur, for inviting me to deliver the GIAN Lectures, eight connected presentations, all relevant to the development of the book. I also wish to thank the faculty of Thomas Jefferson High School (Fairfax, Virginia) for several opportunities to speak to and interact with the world history students. For many years I have presented my developing ideas at the Midwest Institute for community college teachers, based in Kalamazoo, Michigan. Thanks to the arranger, Theo Sypris.

Special thanks to the faculty of my home institution, the Center for South Asian Studies, University of Michigan, for conversations on topics central to the book. The faculty and staff of the libraries at the University of Michigan provided assistance and expertise on dozens and dozens of occasions. The media center staff patiently taught me to use a variety of the latest hardware and software.

Three fellow historians were always willing to discuss ideas of the book, no matter how formless: Richard Tucker, Richard Eaton, and Lee Schlessinger. My brother, Roy Gordon, professor of chemistry and material science at Harvard University, explained the physics and chemistry of glass, one of his specialties.

My editor at Oxford University Press, Charles Cavaliere, remained enthusiastic and insightful through five drafts of the book.

The Fulbright Foundation provided financial support for a year of research on topics relevant to the book. I wrote the final draft as an accompanying dependent during my wife's Fulbright research in India.

Reviewers

Ibrahim Al-Marashi, *California State University San Marcos*

David Atwill, *Penn State University*

Nathan Brooks, *New Mexico State University*

Annette Chapman-Adisho, *Salem State University*

Sean Dunwoody, *Binghamton University*

Erik Eliav Freas, *Borough of Manhattan Community College-CUNY*

Melissa Gayan, *Georgia Southern University*

Kelly Anne Hammond, *University of Arkansas*

Aaron W. Irvin, *Murray State University*

Erik Maiershofer, *Hope International University*

Gary Marquardt, *Westminster College*

Kate McGrath, *Central Connecticut State University*

Michael E. McGuire, *Salem State University*

Julia Osman, *Mississippi State University*

Nicholas Lee Rummell, *Trident Technical College*

Nadejda Williams, *University of West Georgia*

Eric Johnson, *Kutztown University of Pennsylvania*

Walter D. Ward, *University of Alabama at Birmingham*

Mark W. Lentz, *Utah Valley University*

Charles V. Reed, *Elizabeth City State University*

Jon Davidann, *Hawaii Pacific University*

Jason Ripper, *Everett Community College*

About the Author

Stewart Gordon is an independent research scholar associated with the Center for South Asian Studies at the University of Michigan. He has produced several dozen academic books and articles but is anything but a stuffy academic. He has rambled by bus across Turkey, Iran, Afghanistan, Pakistan and India. He has struggled up Inca paths in Peru and boated up the Mekong and the Mississippi. Gordon has served as a consultant for the History Channel, the Discovery Channel, the Walt Disney Company and the American Queen steamboat. He has received many awards including Woodrow Wilson fellowship, a Fulbright fellowship, an Earhart Foundation writing grant, and an Honorary Membership in the Asiatic Society of Mumbai. *A History of the World in Seven Themes* is his ninth book. One of Gordon's previous books, *When Asia Was the World* (2007), has been translated into eight languages.

Gordon has been a professional restorer of fine antique furniture and has owned shops in Ann Arbor, Los Angeles and London. He currently lives in Ann Arbor and has recently built a full-sized, fully equipped horse drawn gypsy wagon (*vardo*). He regularly produces folk art moving sculpture. See StewartGordonHistorian.com

Foreword

In a Time of Pandemic, May 2020

As I complete this manuscript, across much of the world schools, retail shops, movie theaters, restaurants, bars, airlines, and manufacturing industries are closed. People wear facial masks and surgical gloves. My wife and I go out only for groceries, not visiting friends or family. We wait and hope that 20 percent unemployment is not the new norm.

Countries face a common problem: a virus new to humans and for which we have no immunity. Millions are infected and many recover, but the estimates of deaths are already in the millions. We hope the virus can be beaten, but in spite of several effective vaccines a sober view anticipates recurrence of COVID-19 for years.

An *epidemic* is a life-threatening infection that is extremely contagious. Its vector (means of transmittal) can be directly person-to-person (coughing, sex, or touching an infected surface), through an intervening organism (fleas, cows, or mosquitos), or carried by food or drink (tainted water, infected food). Once the pathogen enters the body, it begins to replicate. The outcome for an individual depends how quickly the body can identify the pathogen and how efficiently it can kill infected cells. The outcome for a group depends on the efficiency of the vector. The spread of tuberculosis, for example, generally requires repeated contact with an infected person in the family or at work. Malaria, by contrast, requires only a single bite of a mosquito that has previously bitten an infected person.

The vector of an epidemic is limited by ecological conditions. For example, Rift Valley Fever used to infect and kill cattle and people along the Nile River, but only in years of heavy upstream rain and much standing water downriver. Fortunately, dams along the Upper Nile now control the water in the lower river and the disease has disappeared. Several pathogens, including the virus of the common cold, do not thrive in summer heat and largely disappear from the population only to flare up again in cooler weather.

An epidemic becomes a *pandemic* when the vector is so efficient and the pathogen so effective at commandeering the body that there is no stopping the disease's spread across the world. Particularly devastating are diseases that people have not encountered before, so that their immune system is not primed to do battle.

Epidemics and pandemics have been part of human existence for thousands of years. The Hebrew Bible explicitly mentions plague as one of Yahweh's punishments visited upon Pharaoh's kingdom. Athens suffered a devastating epidemic in the wake of the Peloponnesian War with Sparta (431–404 BCE). The Plague of Justinian (541–550 CE) killed upwards of 25 million in areas that are now the countries of Turkey and Iran and the port cities of the eastern Mediterranean. From these ancient outbreaks to our own time people have suffered through several pandemics and many epidemics: yellow fever, smallpox, bubonic plague, Rift Valley fever, Spanish influenza, mad cow disease, methicillin-resistant staphylococcus aureus (MRSA), AIDS, Ebola, and severe acute respiratory syndrome (SARS).

Until the twentieth century people had no idea what caused epidemics. They had no tools to discover tiny creatures in the water droplets of a cough or flea saliva. Responses to large numbers of people becoming ill and many dying were similar, regardless of religion, language, culture, or region. Those who could fled, but often carried the pathogen to new areas. The rest of the population sealed themselves in their homes or towns, usually passing the disease to family and neighbors. Charlatans sold useless potions, amulets, and herbal cures. People buried their dead and prayed. As they watched their loved ones die, they speculated about the causes of such catastrophes: bad vapors, cold or hot weather, bad water, God's wrath for a lack of faith, the taint of foreigners or hated minorities, the alignment of the stars, the sin of pride, a corrupt and failing dynasty, or the curse of dangerous women.

One of the most-documented pandemics is the Black Plague, which entered Europe in the 1340s, which killed more than 25 million people in Europe alone, one-third of the population. At its peak thousands died every day in major cities, such as Baghdad, Cairo, London, and Paris. No one understood that the vector of the disease was a virus carried in infected fleas on rats.

An eyewitness described the horrors of the Black Plague in France:

> To France, this plague came in a northern direction from Avignon, and
> was there more destructive than in Germany, so that in many places
> not more than two in twenty survived. Many were struck, as if by light-
> ening, and died on the spot, and this more frequently among the young
> and strong than the old; patients with enlarged glands in the axillae

and groins scarcely survived two or three days; and no sooner did these fatal signs appear, than they bid adieu to the world, and sought consolation only in the absolution which Pope Clement VI, promised them in the hour of death.[1]

Epidemiological studies show that the Black Plague did not "end." Smaller outbreaks recurred for centuries. Even today pockets of the Black Plague remain in some groups of prairie dogs. Fortunately, a medicine kills the virus in humans.

Historians have documented major Black Plague effects on the fabric of society. In cities, longstanding hatred of Jews flared into mass killings. Across Europe, the population was so decimated that agricultural labor became scarce and valuable. Peasants rejected bondage to the land and successfully demanded wages for their labor. They also moved to the cities and took up trades. The fear of a recurrence of Black Plague altered the psychology of Europe and the Middle East for centuries. Faith in the Catholic Church was shaken as prayer, vows, and relics proved powerless before the plague. Some people opted for orgies. Others joined traveling bands of penitents, who beat themselves with leather flails.

Between the Black Death and COVID-19 the milestones for understanding epidemics were medical, societal, and technological. The improved lenses of the seventeenth century allowed researchers such as Antonie van Leeuwenhoek to explore the world of germs. In the same century, the Emperor of China observed that a few Chinese doctors introduced cowpox germs into healthy people to prevent smallpox. The emperor, whose father had died of the disease, had his family inoculated and later commanded inoculation for the general population. Travelers brought the idea of inoculation against smallpox to Europe in the eighteenth century. The general idea that a weakened form of a virus stimulated the body to manufacture its own defenses slowly gained acceptance. American presidents were vaccinated and supported general vaccination. Late in the nineteenth century scientists developed vaccines for cholera, anthrax, and diphtheria. Two decades later the same processes produced vaccines for tetanus and diphtheria. Still more recently, in the 1950s, came the vaccine against polio.

In the last two decades an astonishing number of new medicines have appeared in the market, many the result of improved methods of analysis and testing. The CRISPR gene-cutting and splicing system, for example, makes it

---

[1] This description is quoted in J. F. C. Hecker and Henry Morley, *The Black Death and the Dancing Mania*, trans. Guy Babington (n.p.: 1888). A clear transcription of the book is available online at the Gutenberg Project.

relatively easy to remove an undesirable portion of a virus and insert a set of operative genetic material. The virus will still do what it does best, placing its whole gene string inside the cell, where the inserted material manufactures a useful protein or other material. Other sophisticated methods include rapid duplicating of genetic material and programs that image the physical shape of micro-portals and cellular connecting points. New microscopes image ever-smaller sections of pathogens, some microscopes capable of showing the process of infection in real time. Powerful computers are intrinsic to medical break-throughs. One such program, for example, sorts possible cures for a disease by the findings of research on other diseases and ranking a vast number of medicines by the likelihood of being effective on a targeted disease.

To a historian, much of the progress and lethality of COVID-19 seems eerily familiar, like the Black Plague or the Spanish flu of 1919. Much, however, is different. The revolution in information is perhaps the most striking new feature of this pandemic. Governments can in real time track what seems to be working and what does not. The collection of data about where the breakouts occur is updated every day. The gene sequence of the virus was completed within a month of its appearance. Perhaps most striking is a network that connects more than 250 research labs around the world working on a medicine or a vaccine. Unlike any other previous shared venture, thousands of scientists share data as their experiments produce it. This scale of scientific cooperation across national boundaries is a ray of hope in difficult times. These scientific efforts have already produced three successful vaccines and many useful insights into controlling the next pandemic disease, which will surely come. Even though numbers of those infected by COVID-19 are still rapidly rising in many countries, such as India and Brazil, other countries are seeing fewer cases and are opening schools and restaurants.

Our lives have already changed because of COVID-19. Distance learning is the predominant form of education. We keep social distance as normal practice. We decide whether a trip to a big box store is worth the risk. We spend a lot of time on the computer chatting and socializing with friends and family. I truly hope that the themes and processes explored in this volume prove useful in understanding worldwide phenomena such as COVID-19.

A History *of the* World
in Seven Themes

Sex, Sexuality, and Gender

The Big Picture: Society and Gender

Every country issues birth certificates, which register similar information: date and time of birth, attending professional, name of the baby, name of the mother and father, and place of birth. Prominent on most certificates is the question of the sex of the baby. The options are male or female. Essential to our discussion is the difference between sex and gender. Sex is based on physiology, specifically the external and internal genitals. By contrast, gender is the *process* by which a person—within a social group— is channeled and trained to become a man or a woman. The subtle and not-so-subtle training of babies to be boys and eventually men or to be girls and eventually women begins even before birth. In the United States, once ultrasound establishes that the fetus is male or female, the baby's room might well be painted blue or pink, respectively. Parents pick out the baby's first toys, soft plush footballs or soft plush dolls. This process happens whether the family speaks Hungarian or Urdu, practices Christianity or Zoroastrianism, lives in an apartment or a mud hut.

As the researcher Judith Butler has explained, gender is *performed* as a series of small acts that are either approved of or censured by the people present in a child's

An illustration from *The Life of an Amorous Man* (1682) by Ihara Saikaku shows a man using a spyglass to observe a bathing woman.

| 3 |

everyday life. The training on how to become a man or a woman includes sayings and songs by the mother, instruction by the father, approval or disapproval by older siblings, choice of haircut, clothes given to the child, the values embedded in a culture's great sagas, and, later, acceptance or rejection at work or in church.[1] Gendered behaviors are neither arbitrary nor voluntary; they are encoded and expected. The consequences of not performing properly range from teasing to harassment, ostracism, physical abuse, even death. In our own time, gender signals are embedded in television shows, advertising, and other powerful forms of communication. Who is shown taking care of babies, washing dishes, driving the kids to school? What skills does a father teach a son but not a daughter? For millennia, men have wielded enormous power over this gendering process.

There have always been people who could not or would not become the man or woman that society demanded. For many, the awareness of being somehow different started early, described as being in the "wrong body" and uninterested in gender-prescribed activities and attire. As boys, they might want to watch TV shows intended for girls or to learn needlecraft. The first stirrings of sexual interest were also not "appropriate," girls desiring and fantasizing about an older girl or boys having a crush on an older boy. The degree of guilt, fear, and anger depended on the surrounding society's reaction to nonconforming children or teenagers. Over the long sweep of history societies have differed in how they treated such nonconforming people.[2] Were they tolerated, ostracized, imprisoned, declared sick, or perhaps treated as a special, even holy, person? How is our understanding of the world different when it includes gender? How does this thinking affect the present and the future? What does someone mean when promoting a "traditional" family or a "traditional" role for men and women? How do these stereotypes reinforce the power of men as "natural"? Will those on the forefront of today's shifting definitions of gender be more grounded and confident knowing that every permutation and combination of resistance to gender channeling has been explored in earlier human history?

Recent research on nonconforming gender is vast, encompassing literally tens of thousands of books and articles. This chapter focuses on two important elements of the subject, male-male love and sexuality and female-female love and sexuality. Links explore other aspects of gender, such as gender fluidity, class and gender, and whether the terms "gay," "lesbian," and "queer" are useful in describing gender in the past or outside the West.

In this chapter we will take a hopscotching tour of same-sex love and sexuality in a few societies throughout the world in the sixteenth and seventeenth centuries. Our first guide to an exploration of male-male love and sexuality is Ihara Saikaku, a popular Japanese poet and writer, who with wit, irony, and sophistication described the pleasures and problems of the new city-dwellers, a world he knew intimately.

Saikaku and His World

Ihara Saikaku was born in 1642 into a wealthy, educated merchant family in Osaka, a major Japanese seaport and commercial center. He inherited the family business as a late teenager, but within a few years he turned it over to clerks of his father's generation. He married in his late teens, and his wife died when he was only twenty-four. He enjoyed travel and explored many different regions of Japan, noting the area's food, clothes, specialty products, and businesses. He died in 1693, at age fifty-one.[3]

None of these plain facts suggest the dynamic world in which he lived. For centuries families of Japan's powerful samurai (warrior) class had controlled,

Map 1.1

under the nominal lordship of the daimyo (aristocracy), both the land and the social order. Honor and reputation mattered more to samurai families than entrepreneurship or making money. Peasants eked out subsistence and were, in practical terms, bound to the land. Warfare among samurai families was endemic and enormously wasteful of basic resources. Only the conservative courts of the daimyo could afford to patronize artists, craftsmen, and poets, and they set strict conventions for the visual arts and poetry.

All of this changed rapidly in the first half of the seventeenth century. In 1603 the military leader Tokugawa Ieyasu defeated the last of the samurai forces, consolidated power, and founded the Tokugawa Shogunate, a dynastic military government that endured for nearly three centuries. He set about turning his soldiers into administrators and established an enforced peace. External and internal trade grew and generated new wealth, which was concentrated in the rising cities of Edo, Osaka, and Kyoto, not the old landed estates of the daimyo and samurai. Many tradesmen and peasants came from the countryside to find fortune in the cities. The newly rich urban entrepreneurs rejected the highly refined imagery and restrictive conventions of the art and poetry of the former social order in favor of something earthier and more reflective of their life of struggles and pleasures.[4]

Portrait of Tokugawa Ieyasu, founder of the dynasty that ruled Japan from 1603 to 1868.

Our guide, Ihara Saikaku, was a master of haika (linked verse) poetry, but he is justly remembered for the prose form introduced in *The Life of an Amorous Man* (1682). It consisted of thematically linked brief stories, the subject matter of which described his urban world, from the lives of stage actors to the rent on houses.[5] His prose featured short dramatic sentences that were associated by idea or theme rather than by a single overall plot line. What was truly new in Saikaku's prose, however, was an emphasis on the "floating" or transitory nature of life. One could be at the peak of success at one moment but bankrupt the next, as suggested in this incident in a longer story:

> On his way back, Katsuya encountered a strange man at Mimizuka. Traces of the morning's frost had settled on the bamboo bark raincoat the man used as a windbreak, but he seemed unconcerned by it. The man spoke meekly, in a way strangely incongruous with his large stature.
>
> "Excuse me sire, could you spare me a coin?"
>
> When they saw each other face to face, the beggar crouched low and covered his face with his sleeve. Perplexed, Katsuya looked at the man more closely. It was an old compatriot of his, Kataoka Gensuke!
>
> "You look terrible! Katsuya gasped. "Tell me, what happened?"
>
> Gensuke wept as he told his tale.
>
> "I had ambitions and rashly asked for permission from our lord to go to Murakami in Echigo Province to take up a new position. Just when I got there, the man on whom I was dependent for making the final arrangements, Katoaka Genki, died very suddenly. To make matters worse, I have been suffering from an eye ailment since the end of the sixth month last year. I came to Yoshimine, but there was no improvement. My attendants all deserted me, but that was to be expected. They were only temporary hirelings. A man's fate is unpredictable. . . .
>
> "At this point I am thinking of returning to the place of my birth in Nambu where I still have a few connections. After all, I am only 26 years old, and my eyesight has improved enough that I can see your face clearly."[6]

Japanese Buddhist writing of the period acknowledged life's precariousness and recommended detachment from the world of ceaseless change. The new writers of the "floating world" drew exactly the opposite lesson from life's transitory condition, reveling in the chanciness of daily life and promoting sensual pleasure as the only sure reward in an uncertain world. Brothels and theaters were sites where daring same-sex or heterosexual love could be semipublic.

A print showing three courtesans and their attendant crossing a street, early eighteenth century Japan.

To get a sense of the tension between Buddhist spiritualism and the sensuality of the floating world, consider this passage from Saikaku in which two beautiful boy lovers brought a priest, who had turned away from the worldly life, back to worldly desire:

> At about this time, there lived in the far reaches of Shishigatani a Buddhist ascetic who was over 80 years old. They say that from the moment he chanced to see these two splendid boys, his concentration on future salvation failed him and the good deeds he had accumulated in previous incarnations went to naught. News of the priest's feelings reached the boys. Not sure which of them the old gentleman had his heart set on, both went to his rude abode for a visit. Predictably, he found it impossible to dispense with either cherry blossoms or fall foliage. Thus, he satisfied with both of them the love he had harbored from spring to autumn.
>
> The next day, both boys paid another visit to the priest, for there was something they had neglected to tell him, but he was nowhere to be found. They discovered only a poem, dated the previous day, tied to a forked branch of bamboo:

Here are my travel weeds
Tear-stained like my faithless heart
Torn between the two;
I shall cut my earthly ties
And hide myself away in bamboo leaves....

The boys took the bamboo branch and had a skilled artisan make it
into a pair of flutes. On cold winter nights when they played together,
heavenly beings were moved to peek down from the sky.[7]

In the later 1680s Saikaku wrote stories of homosexuality specifically among
the samurai. Despite occasional government bans, homosexuality was longstanding and a significant feature of the samurai code of honor.[8] In practice
the bonds were typically between an older samurai and a younger acolyte, as
an older brother/younger brother relationship. Homosexual ties might also
develop between a daimyo and one of his pages, as well as between young pages
at the same court. Deep love and commitment run through his prose, but
Saikaku also told stories of rivalries for a beautiful page (which sometimes
resulted in deadly dueling), betrayals, and rejections.

Saikaku's *Tales of Samurai Honor* (1687) are frequently ironic, depicting
circumstances in which homosexual love clashes with other parts of the samurai
honor code. One of Saikaku's stories tells of a lord who orders his samurai to
kill a man who is a friend of the samurai, which he does, as his code demands.
Years later, by chance, he meets the widow and her son in a forest far away from
the court. He falls in love with the boy. Two years pass, and suddenly the widow
recognizes her son's lover as the very samurai who had killed her husband. She
demands that her son kill him, and the samurai supports this vengeance. The
son opens his heart to the samurai, explaining how he must kill him, though
he loves him. The widow comes into her son's room and says that she admires
them both:

Each is a man of honor. Love each other for this one night. I wish to
grant you this interval. Celebrate your separation, but tomorrow . . .
avenge your father.

The story ends in the morning. The mother finds the two lovers in close embrace. She calls to awaken them, but both have died from a single sword thrust
by the samurai. The mother then kills herself.[9] Many of these stories end badly,
with a samurai losing his lover because of the violence explicit in his rigid code
of conduct.

The audience for Saikaku's stories was not the samurai but the newly rich
townsmen. For them he wrote an extended and often misogynous book arguing

that homosexual love was superior to heterosexual love, with stories to demonstrate his point. In reality, upper-class male readers of Saikaku's works were much more likely to have been in bisexual relationships, enjoying both men and women.

Babur's "Youthful Follies"

The second stop on our tour is Kabul, the current capital of Afghanistan. Babur (1483–1530), a descendant of the Mongol emperor Ghengis Khan, first raided and then conquered North India. Including Delhi (1519 CE), one of the largest cities in the world, He then married a suitable woman:

> Though I was not ill-disposed toward her, yet, this being my first marriage, out of modesty and bashfulness, I used to see her once in ten, fifteen, or twenty days. Later on when even my first inclination did not last, my bashfulness increased. Then my mother Khalim used to send me [to my wife], once a month or every forty days, with driving and driving, dunnings [demands] and worrying.[10]

He was about to feel a love that overwhelmed him:

> In those leisurely days I discovered in myself a strange inclination . . . for a boy in the camp-bazaar. . . . Up til then I had had no inclination for any-one, indeed of love and desire, either of hear-say or experience, I had not heard, I had not talked. . . .
>
> From time to time Baburi used to come to my presence but out of modesty and bashfulness, I could never look straight at him. . . . In my joy and agitation I could not thank him [for coming]; how was it possible for me to reproach him for going away? . . .
>
> In that frothing up of desire and passion, and under the stress of youthful folly, I used to wander, bare-headed and bare-foot, through street and lane, orchard and vineyard. I showed civility neither to friend nor stranger, took no care or myself or others. . . .
>
> Sometimes like the madmen, I used to wander alone over hill and plain; sometimes I betook myself to gardens and the suburbs, lane by lane. My wandering was not of my choice, and not I decided whether to go or stay.[11]

Written nearly a decade later, Babur's memoir terms this period his "youthful follies" and recounts no later homosexual adventures. When Babur wrote short descriptions of nobles, which he did often, homosexuality was noted, along with a man's cleverness at poetry or predilection for funny practical jokes. Homosexuality certainly was no bar to honorable military service, and it was relatively common and openly practiced. In keeping with the larger Islamic world at the time, however, Babur in his memoir generally frowns on homosexuality and treats it as a something of a character flaw.

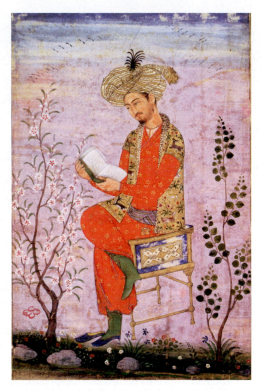

Babur reading. This portrait was painted more than a century after his death in 1530.

Homosexuality in Renaissance Florence

Our next stop is Renaissance Florence around 1500, during Babur's lifetime. Officially, the Church treated sodomy as a mortal sin against faith, reason, nature, society, and the proper ordering of gender.[12] This strident attitude began with Paul's Letter to the Romans (ca. 57 CE):

> [People] exchanged the truth of God for a lie, and worshiped and served the creature rather than the Creator, who is blessed forever. Amen. For this reason God gave them over to degrading passions; for their women exchanged the natural function for that which is unnatural, and in the same way also the men abandoned the natural function of the woman and burned in their desire toward one another, men with men committing indecent acts and receiving in their own persons the due penalty of their error.[13]

Map 1.2

More than a thousand years later Catholic priests still taught this doctrine and featured it in sermons. In Florence, for example, laws required dire punishments for not only sodomy but even for enabling sodomy. An innkeeper who rented rooms where sodomy took place was to have his inn burned down. Despite these laws, in the fourteenth century only about a dozen men per decade were actually convicted for sodomy, usually in conjunction with serious crimes of murder or rape.[14]

Before about the 1450s in Florence homosexual relationships were quite common and well-integrated into society. Like homosexuality in Saikaku's Japan and Babur's Central Asia, homosexual liaisons were generally between an older man (known in court documents as "active") and a boy (usually in his mid- to late teens and known as "passive"). When a boy passed into his twenties, he became the active partner and pursued the next generation of boys. By about age thirty the vast majority of Florentine men were married with children and had turned away from liaisons with boys. Legally and socially there was no suggestion that this pattern somehow reduced a man's masculinity or placed him outside the norms of society.

Scholars know much about homosexual practice in Renaissance Florence because of larger political and religious trends. The Protestant Reformation was taking hold in northern Europe, and the Pope worried that it would sweep through France, Spain, and Italy, the Catholic strongholds. The Pope, therefore, ratcheted up examination and prosecution for heresy and, as part of this campaign, activated

"Two Young Men Embracing" by Bartolomeo Cesi (1556–1629 CE).

the ecclesiastical tribune known as the Inquisition to suppress all aspects of sinful behavior. In 1462, the city council of Florence instituted the "Office of the Night" to arrest homosexuals and vanquish homosexual behavior. The thousands of depositions of men before this court suggest just how common homosexuality was at the time. The court never prosecuted the boys, assuming that they were victims of the older (active) men. In fact, the only prosecutions of older men were those who continued homosexual practice beyond suitable marriageable age, and were therefore considered chronic offenders. The Office of the Night arrested more than 17,000 men in its eighty years of operation and was finally shut down as a failure in 1508 (about a decade before Babur's youthful follies).[15] It is important to note that between 1350 and 1450 wave after wave of the Black Death, a devastating pandemic of bubonic plague, decimated Florence's population, from at least 70,000 to a low point of around 40,000. In the absence of any means to stop these plagues, many blamed them on the immorality of Florence's citizens—hence the support for the Office of the Night.

Gender Channeling in the Americas

Our last stop is in Spanish Florida in 1669 (a couple of decades before Saikaku wrote on homosexuality among the samurai). A Spanish traveler named Francisco Coreal noticed homosexual activity among the natives:

> The men are strongly inclined to sodomy; but the boys that abandon thus are excluded from the society of men and sent out to that of women as being effeminates. . . . they employ them in all the diverse handiwork of women, in servile functions, and to carry munitions and provisions of war. They are also distinguished from the men and women.[16]

Traveling priests and administrators in Central and South America noticed men dressed like women in many indigenous villages. The men participated in women's work teams, occasionally led them and engaged in homosexual

"Natives in Florida Choosing a Bride," by Theodore de Bry, ca. 1598 CE.

activity. They did not seem to have any special spiritual role, but they did have a ritual one. In some areas, Inca high administrators (curacas) sexually penetrated them during ceremonies, apparently demonstrating their submission. There is evidence that in some parts of Central and South America young nobles had sex with them in order to avoid fights over available local women. None of the Spanish sources suggest that a young boy chose to be a feminized submissive man. The Spanish generally attributed this phenomenon to the "work of the Devil" and, for centuries, no one paid much attention to this stable and locally accepted gender channeling.[17]

Male-Male Love from a Global Perspective

From our hopscotching tour thus far, the most important point is that the terms heterosexual and homosexual are modern constructions and not somehow natural and universal categories. Many sixteenth- and seventeenth-century societies disapproved of male-male love and sexual relations but varied hugely in the degree they cared about, actively opposed, or demonized such behavior. Among the large world religions, Christianity most consistently demonized same-sex love and used ecclesiastical courts and church power to suppress male-male love as a crime against nature, society, and God.[18] At the time of our tour, Church writing had hardened to the point of demanding the death penalty for such practices. By contrast, the Confucianism and Taoism of China did not, on the whole, single out male-male love for condemnation. Confucianism did not find that male-male love disrupted effective working of the state, which was its main concern. Taoism did not believe that male-male love affected the energy flows and connections to nature central to its beliefs. In fact, at the time of our tour, deep love between males as mentors and friends was a pervasive theme in Chinese literature, theater, and visual arts. Buddhism of this period disapproved of male-male love as one among many of the "attachments" that hindered the practitioner from reaching the "detached" state of nirvana. Judaism would seem to be unambiguously opposed to male-male love based on the prohibition in Leviticus 20:13:

> If a man lies with a male as with a woman, both of them have commit-
> ted an abomination; they shall surely be put to death; their blood is
> upon them.

In reality, discreetly practiced male-male love was generally ignored. The same was true for Islam. The Qur'an recounts the story of the destruction of "the people of Lot" because of male-male sex and love. Over centuries of actual practice, however, Islamic courts rarely punished such love. Literature and art celebrated it. Babur's mild disapproval of his own youthful follies seems a common attitude in this period of Islam.

Also noteworthy, we found that men in several societies shifted between alternate gender roles. As teens, they were the passive (penetrated) receiver of an active older man (penetrator, mentor, teacher). The teen grew into the role of an active and, by his thirties, usually was married with children. This pattern has appeared in a variety of societies, such as ancient Greece and Rome, Renaissance Italy, and medieval Buddhist monasteries in Japan.

Researchers try to understand these long-ago relationships from relatively indirect evidence: laws, court cases, literature, folk tales, and artwork. Until the nineteenth century, letters of male-male love were rare and memoirs were even rarer. The evidence is incomplete and suggestive rather than conclusive. The evidence of male-male love is, nevertheless, far richer than the few early mentions of female-female love, to which we now turn.

Female-Female Love and Sexuality

Male-male love and sexual activity are everywhere in Ihara Saikaku's many tales of the floating world of urban Japan in the sixteenth century. By contrast, he mentions female-female love and sexual relations only once in his vast oeuvre. In one of his stories, the heroine becomes a prostitute in a female-female brothel. Other Japanese writers of the time mention such brothels, and a portion of the Edo brothel district was reserved for female-female houses of prostitution.[19] This evidence supports the existence of female-female love and sexuality, but it is frustratingly lacking in detail. The problems of historical research on female-female love in this early period include meager evidence (reflecting a more general erasure of women in historical records), records overwhelmingly produced by men, and a viewpoint hostile to female-female love and sexuality.[20]

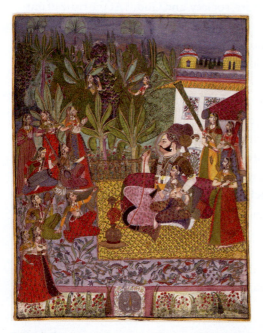

A Mughal prince enjoys a musical performance by the girls of his harem. His much smaller wife nestles next to him, ca. 1770, Jodhpur, northern India.

Love in a Mughal Harem?

Despite the scant documentation, let us continue our hopscotching journey. Our next stop is India, at the court of Mughals, the dynasty established by Babur, he of youthful follies. As we have seen, so long as a man fulfilled his familial obligations of supporting his family and procreating sons, he was largely free to pursue male-male love and sexuality if he so desired. But was the same true for female-female love and sexuality? Our Western fantasy image is of women in a harem, perhaps languorously reclining around an indoor bath. Western artists created these sorts of images, with their suggestions of female-female love, for a European male market, however. The reality for women, even queens, was quite different. Documents of the early Mughals (Babur and his son Humayan) portray a world of constant danger, betrayal, and royal competition. Respite from war was rare; suffering of both men and women was an everyday reality. In good times, queens might have a tent of their own. In defeat, queens and female relatives scattered to what security they could find among their own relatives. Many royal and noble wives did not survive the forced marches of retreat or the diseases of the camp.[21] Female-female love probably happened anyway, but it bore no resemblance to the languorous, erotic harem of Western male fantasy and art.

All-women institutions common in Europe, such as schools, convents, and prisons, did not exist in Mughal society and could not provide a locus for female-female love and sexuality. Even when the Mughals settled in Delhi, royal and noble wives and close female relatives were fully involved in the alliances, power struggles, factions, and revolts typical of the Mughal Empire, all from a *harem*. Wives represented an alternate basis for the legitimacy of strategic alliances.[22] The writings of the time document a clear hierarchy of wives and female relatives (based, in part, on their production of male heirs).[23] Could the harem also have been a site of female-female love and romance? We do not know. The only evidence is Urdu poetry known as *rekhti*, a genre begun decades after Babur, which uses women's voices to talk about themselves, often on the topic of longing for the beloved. Some poems are quite explicit:

> When you join your lips to my lips,
> It feels as if new life pours into my being,
> When breast meets breast, the leisure is such
> That from sheer joy the words rise to my lips.
> The way you rub me, ah! It drives my heart wild
> Stroke me a little more, my sweet Dogana[24]

"Dogana" plays on the word "do," which implies "twoness," an intimate joining of "two of the same."

These poems are not statements by women, however. To the contrary, men wrote the poems and performed them for elite male audiences. Just to complicate matters, the poet sometimes performed *rekhti* poems dressed as a woman. We can say for sure that the *rekhti* poets must have known women who practiced female-female love, as the details they relay are intimate and accurate.[25] Twentieth-century prudishness erased the entire genre from anthologies of historical Urdu poetry.[26]

The Inquisition of Benedetta Carlini

The next stop is a return to Florence a few decades after the closure in 1508 of the Court of the Night. The Court may have ended, but the Inquisition remained active. The accused was Benedetta Carlini, born of relatively wealthy parents in a small village about forty-five miles northwest of Florence. At birth, she was dedicated to the Church and entered the religious life at age nine at Pescia, down the mountain from her birthplace.[27] At age twenty-one, Benedetta began having visions of Jesus, holy gardens, and angels. Were the visions sent by God or the devil? Her confessor was skeptical of her apparitions and advised that only suffering would clarify they truly came from God. For several years she lived with severe joint and muscular pain, and in dreams she repeatedly cast out the devil in the form of a handsome young man. The convent gradually accepted Benedetta's trances and visions as genuine communications from God, and its leaders felt honored to have her. One night, she manifested the stigmata (bodily wounds corresponding to the crucifixion wounds of Jesus Christ) on her body; all doubts were overcome. Some months later she symbolically married Jesus at the altar of the convent with all the nuns in attendance. They, however, did not see what she saw: Jesus and the heavenly host (God's holy angels). Doubts slowly proliferated, and Church investigators began a series of visitations to the convent. They believed the nuns who reported seeing Benedetta use a large needle to create the stigmata and her own blood to decorate her wedding ring.

What finally destroyed Benedetta's credibility as a mouthpiece of God was the deposition of Sister Bartolomea Crivelli. She had been assigned as Benedetta's companion to minister to her during pains and violent dreams. According to the account she told the investigators:

> For two continuous years, at least three times a week, in the evening after disrobing and going to bed would wait for her companion to disrobe, and pretending to need her, would call. When Bartolomea would come over, Benedetta would grab her by the arm and throw her by force on the bed. Embracing her, she would put her under herself and kissing

her as if she were a man, she would speak words of love to her. And she would stir on top of her so much that both of them corrupted themselves. And thus by force she held her sometimes one, sometimes two, and sometimes three hours.[28]

This crime was apparently so heinous and unusual that precedents were rare. Skeptical that she was an unwilling victim, the investigators questioned Sister Bartolomea as to why she had not resisted or called out or told other nuns. She said that Benedetta told her that she came to her as an angel named Splenditello and, indeed, Benedetta's voice and manner changed during the trysts. The investigators submitted their report, but papal attention was lacking and action on the case stalled. Years passed.

The papal nunzio finally sent its own investigator to the convent, who found that Benedetta had neither stigmata nor a ring of Jesus. Her manner was suitably demure, however, and the papal investigator accepted Benedetta's assertion that possession by the devil had caused all of her transgressions and that the devil no longer controlled her. Nevertheless, three years later she was sentenced to life imprisonment for her sins and spent thirty-five years in solitary confinement. Only in death did she return to her convent for burial.

Like nearly all societies in the time of our tour, the sixteenth and seventeenth centuries in Renaissance Florence was a patriarchal society—that is, controlled by men for the advantages that it bestowed on men. Many aspects of the control of women by men directly impacted female-female love: required dress, household seclusion, unavailability of independent income, inheritance laws that excluded women, lack of access to the legal system, prohibition of education, no choice of sexual partner, required production of male children, and banning of women from strength and self-defense training. Any "mannish" dress or actions threatened the whole patriarchal edifice, and the surrounding society knew it. In Holland at this time, for example, it was a serious offence for a woman to wear men's clothes, punishable by a long prison term.

Two-Spirits Among First Nations Americans

The last stop on our tour is a return to the United States and the question of "third gender." As we have seen, in the sixteenth century Spanish travelers observed feminized men working with and mainly associating with women. So did twentieth-century European and American anthropologists, who studied First Nations tribes. For a short period it seemed that they had located a practice common to all First Nations, a cultural trait that spanned North, Central, and South America and had a deep history. There was even a term, *berdache*, for these feminized men. It was not, however, an indigenous term but rather a French one. The word's history went back through medieval French to a Persian word for slave.[29]

Recent research has demonstrated that the commonalities of a third gender across the New World were more imagined (by anthropologists) than real. In some tribes a feminized man resulted from a profoundly important teenage vision quest. In other tribes, however, there was no vision quest. In some tribes the feminized man was assumed to have exceptional talents, and in others they had no such talents. It was the same with special spiritual powers and ceremonial responsibilities: true for some tribes and not for others. Some tribes had tests to make sure that a young boy was, in fact, feminized. Others had none. Some tribes required feminized men to wear special clothing. Others did not. Nowhere on the North American continent did early travelers notice the submission practice of the Inca from South America. In some tribes feminized men married, and in others they did not.

Our guide to the concept of third gender is Ma-Nee Chacaby, whom we know about because an American anthropologist named Mary Louisa Plummer befriended her, recorded her stories, and reworked them into a narrative of her life. Ma-Nee was born in 1950 in a remote First Nations encampment a hundred miles north of the Canadian shore of Lake Superior. Some men tended traps

Two-Spirited elder and writer Ma-Nee Chacaby in a pride parade, 2019.

and sold furs; others logged for a timber and paper-pulp company. Ma-Nee's family paddled hundreds of miles each summer, drying fish and berries. From a very early age Chacaby refused to wear the skirts of a Cree girl, dressing instead in a pair of heavy bloomers, which she treated like pants.[30] She liked exploring the nearby forest alone. Her grandmother, a storyteller, raised Ma-Nee and told her that she was a "two-spirit" person, with both a female and a male aspect:[31]

> My grandmother told me that two-spirit, same sex couples used to play an important role in Anishinaabe communities, because they adopted children who had lost their parents. Sometimes, she said, individuals with two spirits had other special duties, like keeping fire, healing people, or leading ceremonies. My *kokum* [grandmother] explained the two-spirit were once loved and respected within our communities, but times had changed and they were no longer understood or valued in the same way.[32]

Ma-Nee began to dress like men of the encampment: checkered lumberjack shirt, jeans, black rubber boots, and a cap.[33] She wanted to look and dance like her idol Elvis Presley. Her first sexual longings were for an older girl, but she did not understand them. During her teenage years more immediate problems overshadowed any difficulties of Ma-Nee's sexual identity as two-spirit. Alcoholism was rampant. Sexual abuse and rape were common, and she experienced both. Ma-Nee remembers that her mother beat her severely and regularly. Still, she learned how to make clothes from her mother and soon fashioned pants and jackets to her liking.[34] From her stepfather Ma-Nee learned skills normally taught only to boys, such as hunting and trapping by dog sled in the winter, catching fish in the summer, and making snowshoes and arrows. He showed her the ceremony to honor the spirit of an animal killed.

Ma-Nee's grandmother predicted that her life as a two-spirit would be hard, and she was right. Ma-Nee was only sixteen when her mother insisted that she marry a man twenty years older. She survived his abuse as well as her own addiction to alcohol and drugs, tuberculosis, and lack of education to emerge as an elder of the Cree tribe. She followed her feelings and shifted to loving women, ultimately finding a long-term cherished companion.

What is important here is that to describe Ma-Nee as a "lesbian" is true but incomplete. She is also a tribal elder, a trained alcohol counselor, a mother to both her own children and others she has taken in, a social reformer both for her tribe and the larger society, a dynamic speaker, and a loving partner. Her various identities jostle within her and compete for time, resources, action, and advocacy. By the end of Plummer's story of her life, Ma-Nee seems content with who and what she is and even the contradictions of her various roles. Male-male and female-female relationships do not (and did not) isolate people

Map 1.3

from the surrounding society. To the contrary, nonconforming people—in secret or in public—have been students, teachers, relatives, friends, coworkers, and fellow citizens, all deeply integrated into their society.[35]

The Bigger Picture

Gender Channeling

In considering sex and gender, the most significant question to ask of past or present societies is if they recognized that sex is not the same thing as gender. Sex is about observed genitalia, while gender describes the reinforcements and punishments that teach a boy to become a man and a girl to become a woman. Some past societies recognized this crucial distinction between sex and gender, but none faced the strength and vibrancy of today's many LGBTQ (lesbian/gay/bisexual/transgender/queer) movements. Young people all over the world are redefining gender. Here are some major themes of the process.

No Simple Categories

When assigning gender to a person, societies have generally preferred the stark categories, based on physical sexual differences, of male or female, but gender has never been that simple. Gender is a social construct: there is nothing natural or inevitable about what a boy or man is supposed to be and do or what a girl or woman is supposed to be and do. Gender channeling has differed throughout history and still varies enormously across the world. We can never assume, for example, that homosexual behavior has always been shameful, transgressive, and punished, as it has generally been in Christian societies. As we have seen, in Japan among the seventeenth-century samurai, the most conservative and honor-bound segment of the society practiced same-sex love.

Power and Class

Gender channeling has always been closely associated with power. Patriarchy not only demanded that women be subordinate to men but also generated very real punishments for challenging or breaking the rules. Readers should recall that only two generations ago (ask your grandmother) a married woman in the United States could not get a credit card or a bank account without the signed agreement of her husband. Women drivers were mocked as incompetent and dangerous.

The channeling of gender has always varied by class. What was expected of an upper-class man or woman was hugely different from what was expected of peasants, workers, or the poor. At its simplest, upper-class people could often defy the expected gender expectations and get away with it. This is, however, not the whole picture. Poor women sometimes "passed" as men in order to qualify for better jobs, such as a soldier, sailor, or cowboy. During the manpower shortage of World War II millions of women took up factory work. The crucial importance of their work for the war effort was not lost on the women involved, and it is no surprise that their daughters grew up to become the leaders in a new wave of feminist organizing.

Nonconformance

Current research suggests that high levels of in utero testosterone can produce babies with ambiguous genitalia as well as children who cannot and will not live as society demands based on their sexual organs. Nonconforming children know and feel who they truly are long before puberty. As young as three or four years old, they prefer "inappropriate" dress, toys, and games. Boys enjoy putting on dresses; girls want to play with trucks and wear only pants. The vast majority of these children are not "going through a phase," but will be transgender for their entire life. The degree of pain, shame, and anger they feel depends on how early and thoroughly the family recognizes and accepts their child as transgender.

Gender and Globalization

At the time of Saikaku and Babur, it was still possible to consider gender within a single society or culture. Travelers noticed that men and women dressed a certain way in Turkey or Morocco or China. In some places men did the weaving, and in other places women did the weaving. All of this was soon to change. By 1750 Europeans conquered nearly the entire world. The conquerors brought their notions of gender and sexuality to their colonies. Ideas of masculinity and femininity mixed and clashed with ideas of gender, race, and class both in the new colonies and in the colonizing countries: Spain, Portugal, England, France, Holland, Russia, and later Belgium, Italy, Germany, and the United States. Gender channeling became more complex as Europeans settled in their colonies. Whose gender norms were to dominate the raising of children of mixed-race families? Were women native to the colonies entitled to the same rights as women in the colonizing country? Would the religion of the colonizers affect the colonized society's established forms

TIMELINE

ca. 57 CE
Paul's Letter to the Romans

1350–1450
Bubonic plague decimates Florence; population reduced from 70,000 to 40,000

ca. 1450
Homosexual relationships are common and well-integrated in Florence society

1462–1508
City council of Florence institutes Office of the Night to vanquish homosexual behavior

1483–1530
Life of Babur

1519
Babur conquers Kabul

1603
Tokugawa Ieyasu defeats the last of the samurai forces and creates the Tokugawa Shogunate

of gender channeling?[36] Did the mix of cultures in a newly colonial society loosen gender channeling?[37]

Visible Communities

Over the centuries between our chapter guides Babur and Ma-Nee Chacaby, one of the biggest changes is nonconforming people organizing themselves into support and ultimately political organizations.[38] These organizations can help hold off the despair of feeling trapped by a binary definition of gender; indeed, they celebrate gender fluidity. In a directly related development, the internet allows linkages among people who cannot or will not live as society demands. Marches and celebrations bring new demands for the human rights of those who do not conform to gender expectations. Acknowledgment of gender fluidity by no means is on the rise worldwide, but for many in the West this is a time of rapid change and social acceptance of all variations of gender.

For digital learning resources, please go to
www.oup.com/he/gordon-seventhemes1e

1642–1693
Life of Ihara Saikaku

1669
Francisco Coreal notices homosexual activity among natives in Spanish Florida

1682
Saikaku writes *The Life of an Amorous Man*

1687
Saikaku writes *Tales of Samurai Honor*

1950
Ma-Nee is born in a First Nations encampment

2016
A Two-Spirit Journey: The Autobiography of a Lesbian Ojibway-Cree Elder is published

Nations and Nationalism

The Big Picture: What Is a Nation?

We all live in countries that we call nations. What and who constitutes a nation would seem to be obvious. The US Declaration of Independence, after all, opens with, "When in the course of human events, it becomes necessary for one people to sever the political bonds which have connected them with another." Chapter 1 of the charter of the United Nations features the "self-determination of peoples." Would that the issue was simple, but it is not. Political scientists, anthropologists, sociologists, historians, lawyers, politicians, and government agencies have produced literally hundreds of books on nationalism—at base, identification with one's own nation and support for its interests—without agreement on even a definition of a people or a nation, much less how nations came into being, when they did so, and how they work.[1] There is no consensus on whether only one kind of nation and nationalism exists—or many kinds. Are nations mainly a physical phenomenon (museums, battlefields, national highways) or mainly a mental phenomenon (national symbols, a shared language, a feeling of loyalty)?[2] Who decides when some people constitute a nation? Do nations automatically have rights, or must they struggle and seize those rights?

Drafting the Declaration of Independence, 1776.

Thinking through the complicated issue of nations, nationalism, and loyalty might begin with a simpler question: What would an ideal nation look like? Here there seems to be some consensus. Within a clearly demarcated, indivisible geographic area all the people of an ideal nation would speak the same language, write in that language; have common customs, ceremonies, music, dress, and cuisine; agree on important events of their history and a vision of the future; school their children with the same values and curriculum; worship alike; share the same conception of proper political organization; form a constituted taxation and governance unit called a nation-state (or nation); and mobilize its population to support and defend that nation-state. Loyalty to the nation would supersede all other loyalties, such as to community, city, religion, and family. Each person would be a citizen of only one nation.[3]

In the long sweep of history, no political state has come even close to this ideal of a nation. In practice, every ethnic or religious group holds competing loyalties. Why should someone be loyal to something larger than his or her immediate family? Why should anyone acknowledge a law code or any higher authority? In the ancient world, the answer to these questions generally emerged from the relations of humans with a powerful divine entity (or entities), such as the god-kings of ancient Egypt, Africa, and Mexico; the almighty Thor and the other Norse gods; the divine ancestors of the aborigines of Australia; and Yahweh, god of the Jews. Belief in divine entities gave a compelling reason for submission to commandments or codes. The community of believers supported one another through good times and bad and defined loyalty in terms of personal moral behavior and the general ordering of society. The believing community asserted that loyalty to its laws, strictures, and commitments superseded all other allegiances.

Some places in the ancient world generated moral codes and loyalty without a divine entity. The Confucian code of moral behavior and the proper ordering of society in China, Korea, and Japan, for example, did not rest on divine authority. Neither did early Buddhism, which was a moral code based on a path to insight, not the worship of any entity. Philosophers in ancient Greece discussed the proper ordering of society independent of any divinity or divine plan, just as Romans did not base their laws on divine inspiration.

With or without a divine basis, group self-identification was not nationalism. The Jews of the Old Testament, for example, saw themselves as different from people around them. Jews had a common language, both written and oral, a shared religion, and occasionally a homeland. They were, nevertheless, deeply divided over their interpretation of religious texts and their day-to-day customs, prayers, and practices, in addition to their views on who should govern and how the homeland should be defended. In similar fashion, scholars have argued that the citizens of Rome formed a self-aware group who promoted unifying customs and ceremonies, formed governing bodies, spoke the same language, and had clear ideas of borders. None of this should be construed as nationalism. Rome never solved the ongoing problem of the many groups within the empire who did not accept this Romanizing process. Thus, many scholars of nationalism accept older forms of group self-identification, but only outliers would term them nations.[4]

The idea of the nation rose in the eighteenth-century West from the interaction of four unique historical processes. The first was philosophical writing, particularly in Germany, that both recognized and celebrated a people as an organic whole: Immanuel Kant, Johann Fichte, and Georg Hegel were leaders in this endeavor. This position challenged the view of political philosophers like John Locke, Jean-Jacques Rousseau, and Adam Smith, who saw each person as an atomized and singular entity, making individual economic and political choices and fitting almost mechanically into the state.[5] Second, writers in France in the decades leading up to the French Revolution (1789–1799) expanded on the themes of a people, rather than the king, as the ultimate source of a state's legitimacy.[6] The idea of a nation's right and responsibility to reject unjust political authority—the nation's self-determination—was discussed, debated, challenged, fought over, and largely adopted in France by the end of the Revolution.[7] Earlier, Great Britain's North American colonies had actively participated in these debates, which underlay the American Revolution (1775–1783). The very process of setting up state institutions, such as a citizen army and a system of taxation, favored the development of nationalism.[8] Third, the idea of the nation traveled easily because industrial print technology developed rapidly in Europe in the second half of the eighteenth century. It generated an explosion of newspapers, books, maps that showed national boundaries, inexpensive woodcuts, etchings, and lithographic images. Political cartoons and metaphorical images of the nation soon followed. Fourth, it is critical to keep in mind that nationalism was not merely a set of debated and discussed ideas. It was at the core of all-too-real wars across the world that broke out in the nineteenth century, such as Norway's repeated attempts to break free from Sweden, Greece's rebellions against Ottoman Turkey, South American revolutions against Spain, and Italy's consolidation of its many competing states. These nationalist movements and wars responded to local and regional conditions and looked just as different from one another in the nineteenth century as historians find them today. Russian nationalism, for example, featured close ties between the people and their church and their czar, while German nationalism moved quickly from recovery of German folk tales and legends to unification consolidation of the small Germanic states and warfare on the periphery, such as the conquest of Sweden.

No nation has a conveniently simple glorious past that all citizens can embrace. This past must be created by highlighting certain events and suppressing others. Can a nation accommodate people who do not share the glorified past? How are most nations to deal with a colonial past that denied citizenship to its subject population? Can

A plate commemorating the execution of Louis XVI on January 21, 1793 during the French Revolution.

nationalists find symbols to which citizens respond? How about people in a nation who speak a different language from or know little of the dominant culture? What is a nation to do about a group actively seeking independence? How much is nationalism implicated in warfare and conflict?

This chapter treats the challenges of nationalism from a global perspective. Our guide is Jomo Kenyatta, who participated in the first stirrings of nationalism in East Africa, became aware of other nationalist movements of the nineteenth and twentieth centuries, and also learned firsthand the problems of creating a nation out of European-dominated colonies. Kenyatta lived long enough to become Kenya's first prime minister when the colony gained its freedom from Britain in 1963.

Colonial Land Grab

Kenyatta's people were the Kikuyu, small farmers and herders in the rolling foothills of Mount Kenya, the second highest mountain in Africa. Volcanic activity thrust up Mount Kenya some three million years ago, but it has been inactive since. Some archaeological evidence supports oral tradition that the Kikuyu came to Mount Kenya (located about 150 miles north of Nairobi) around 300 CE, as part of large migrations of the Bantu peoples. Oral tradition asserts that the Kikuyu were never conquered, though cattle raids and border warfare with the Masai, nomadic herders of the savannah to the south of Mount Kenya, were endemic.[9] The Kikuyu currently number about 6.6 million people, the largest of Kenya's forty-two recognized tribes.

By the time Kenyatta was born (historians estimate ca. 1897, though there are no documents of his birth), the European powers—most notably, Great Britain, France, Germany, and Belgium—had completed the Berlin conference (1884–1885), which divided Africa into "spheres of influence." The conference set arbitrary colonial boundaries, within which each European power could

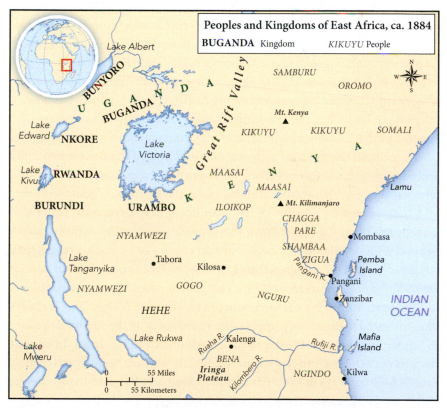

Map 2.1

act without interference from any other European power. The British got what is today Kenya and Uganda. The conference had certainly not consulted or included any African tribal elders.

On the ground, the British land grab had two motivations. White explorers asserted that the land of current-day Uganda and Kenya had huge potential for profitable farming. They declared the region "empty" except for some inconvenient natives. At odds with this white settler view, Christian missionaries had established a few outposts in British East Africa, and the new British colonial administration saw support of their mission as part of its "civilizing" role.

Railways and Colonial Development

At the Berlin conference, the European powers committed to "developing" their spheres of influence, specifically to push railroads into their new colonies. Some of Kenyatta's earliest memories were of the coming of the railroad. The British colonial government took over the failed efforts of a private railway company and in 1895 laid the first rails inland from the port of Mombasa. A few years later the railroad cut across Kikuyu lands. The iron tracks came from Birmingham, England, even though Kikuyu had smelted iron for millennia. The construction workers were contract labor from India. Mules were imported from Cyprus. Rail guards carried repeater rifles, while Kikuyu had only poisoned arrows. A year later the British East African colonial government brought a regiment across the Indian Ocean from British colonial India to put down a rebellion in Uganda. Crucial to understanding nationalism in colonies is the simple fact that European empires were *conquest* empires built on a foundation of violence and the threat of violence. No ruler invited the British to occupy and administer his kingdom because they were better administrators. Kenyatta later wrote of the rail line from Mombasa to inland Uganda as "going nowhere" and "not wanted by anyone." Railway building was a common activity of European colonial governments, the expense justified by administrative necessity. First, railroads connected distant regions of a colony. Second, they triggered rapid economic growth by carrying produce and products of interior farms and mines to urban markets. Third, their often unacknowledged but most important function was to move troops rapidly to quash rebellion. Railways demonstrated their military importance in suppressing the Mahdi Rebellion in Upper Egypt (1881–1889) and the Rebellion of 1857 in India. In the last decades of the nineteenth century and the first decades of the twentieth century France built railways in West Africa and in Vietnam; Belgium in the Congo; and Britain in Canada, East and South Africa, Egypt, and India.

Workers load logs in Cameroon, West-Central Africa, 1917.

Many of these rail lines lost money but still transferred wealth from the colony to the "home" European power. Colonial governments generally guaranteed the return to investors who bought railway bonds, constituting a large-scale transfer of wealth from a colony to the home country. Besides guaranteed bonds, colonial railways transferred wealth from the colonies to the home country in other ways. The railways lines purchased all of their manufacturing material—everything from locomotives to bridges to crockery in the dining cars—from businesses in the home country. The whole upper staff of the railway companies, including high-level executives, stationmasters, and engineers, were from the home country. All were paid from a colony's taxes, as were their pensions, which they received and spent in the home country.

More generally, large-scale public works figure prominently in the mental image of the nation. For instance, the driving in of the Golden Spike in Utah in 1869, which celebrated the completion of the first rail line across the United States, is a common image in American history textbooks. Another example of infrastructure supporting the idea of the nation is the Interstate Highway System in the United States. The 1956 Congressional bill funding the system was titled the "National System of Interstate and Defense Highways," and like

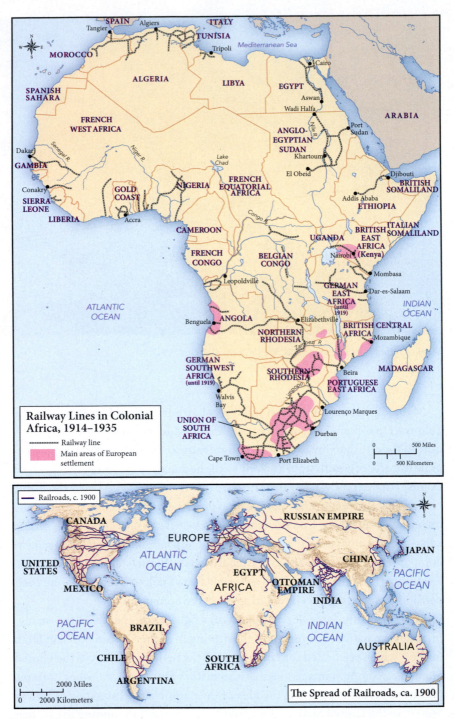

Railway Lines in Colonial Africa, 1914–1935

- - - - - Railway line

Main areas of European settlement

The Spread of Railroads, ca. 1900

Railroads, c. 1900

Map 2.2

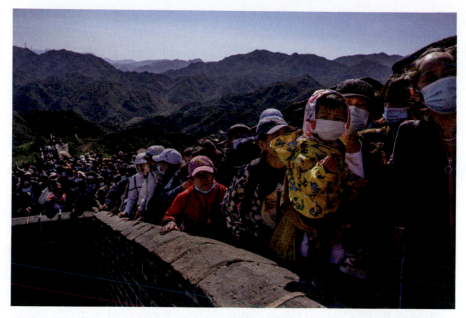

Tourists crowd the Great Wall during the Golden Week government holiday, which encourages travel within China.

the colonial rail line of Kenyatta's childhood was primarily about moving troops and connecting far-flung parts of the nation. The Great Wall of China, built over centuries at enormous human cost, was intended to keep out invaders from inner Asia. It failed, as do most fortified walls, but it remains a powerful symbol of the nation. Today, the Great Wall's image is printed on Chinese postage stamps, and surviving portions of the Wall are much promoted as tourist destinations, especially for Chinese visitors.

Missions and Names

Jomo Kenyatta's birth name was Kamau wa Ngengi, a Kikuyu name meaning that he was Kamau who "belonged" to Ngengi, who had taken him in after his father died. At about age twelve (1909) Kamau saw colonial proclamations posted in his Kikuyu area and decided he wanted to understand the strange marks on the paper. One day a Christian evangelist arrived at Kamau's village from a mission named Thogoto, about twenty-five miles away. Kamau and a friend of the same age decided to join some 250 Kikuyu who lived in simple houses near the mission. Kamau wanted to learn the magic of the marks on paper. He washed dishes, weeded the garden, learned to sew, and eventually apprenticed as a carpenter. By the start of World War I in 1914 Kamau had professed his commitment to the mission's catechism and adapted to a British-style school life of cold showers and hard work.

He also participated in a Kikuyu group circumcision ceremony, which marked him for full participation in adult tribal ritual, landholding, and marriage. Such straddling of the Kikuyu world and the Christian missionary world was common at the time. Missionary students and adults often returned to their villages for months at a time. Kamau was not close to his extended Kikuyu family, but he also saw little prospects at the mission. His English was meager and his carpentry mediocre. In 1914 he left the mission, never to return.

In the decade before the outbreak of World War I, white settlers seized most of the tribal lands of Kenya and forced the tribes onto *shamba* (reservations). White settlers regularly rounded up men from the shamba to work their farms. With the eruption of World War I, the situation of the native tribes further deteriorated.[10] Colonial troops commandeered native men in the thousands and forced them to carry the materials of war to wherever they were needed. More than 100,000 Kenyan natives served in appalling conditions of slavery—ill fed, unprotected from heat and rain, brutally treated, and without medical care. Records are incomplete, but 50,000 men may have died in this forced service. During such military slavery Kamau's younger brother died, undocumented.

The only means to escape this slavery was to seek shelter with the Masai, a tribe that simply refused to become slave labor and backed their opposition with spears. The colonial government did not have the soldiers to fight World War I and simultaneously defeat the Masai. Thus many Kikuyu migrated south into Masai territory. Kamau chose this path and acted as an agent for the purchase of cattle taken to Nairobi as food for troops.

After the war Kamau migrated to Nairobi, which had rapidly grown from a swampy outpost into a booming railway town. Some contract workers from India did not go home at the end of their commitment, but instead they opened small shops in Nairobi. So did men who survived the wartime military slavery but saw wider horizons than returning to their tribal lands. Kamau decided that he needed a new name, one that downplayed his Kikuyu origins and signaled his mission background and his knowledge of English. From Kamau wa Ngengi he became "K. N. Johnstone," and launched himself into the possibilities of Nairobi. Through a white mentor he secured a good job in the water department of Nairobi and opened a shop and pool hall. He married and built a small house on a plot of land near the water department offices. Within a few years Kamau evolved into quite the man about town, quickly making friends with other entrepreneurial, mission-trained natives. They went to movies, drank in bars, and attended soccer games and concerts.

Just as Johnstone's name now suggested connections to white society, so did his dress. He bought used European clothing in the markets and dressed on formal occasions in a suit, tie, and hat. We know his dress because in Nairobi photographic portraits became wildly popular after World War I. Several photographs of K. N. Johnstone and his wife survive. In one he wears a bush jacket and riding breeches and carries a long whip. In another he poses in a military uniform and riding boots.

Portrait of Jomo Kenyatta, first President of Kenya. Note the addition of a beaded cap, not present in other post-Independence photographs.

These changes of name and dress matter because nationalism requires belief that loyalty to the nation supersedes all other loyalties. Such a belief does not come in a flash of insight but instead grows incrementally through personal experience of discrimination, study of nationalism in other countries and colonies, and talk on the subject with friends. The early results of these new influences generally produced a weakening of competing loyalties to, for example, family, community, and religion. In the process of becoming nationalists, men and women experimented with new identities, including different clothing, food, and names. For example, Ho Chi Minh (1890–1969), the leader of Vietnam's uprising against the French and later the United States, used at least a half dozen different names over his long political career. The Indian nationalist leader Mohandas (Mahatma, "great-souled") Gandhi (1869–1948) is remembered as wearing simple native clothing, but Gandhi in his professional career as a young lawyer dressed in tailored suits. Even though his caste was strictly vegetarian, in England he tried meat. On his return to India in 1914 Gandhi stopped wearing suits and instead wore the traditional white clothes of his region and caste. In 1921, he adopted the unsewn wrapped loincloth as a mark of identification with India's rural poor; the loincloth was his signature garment for the rest of his life. Joseph Juggashvili became Joseph Stalin (Stal means "steel" in Russian) two decades before he became the ruthless leader of Russia.

War and Nationalism

World War I changed much in Kenya. A new sense of the whole of one's tribe arose; Kikuyu from a distant ridge were not enemies but had common interests, the same concerns, and a shared identity. The Kikuyu were not yet talking about independence or freedom, but they had suffered and died for the war effort and wanted some compensation. Other grievances were immediate and pressing. During the war, white settlers had been especially active in rounding up Kikuyu men for their plantations, leaving families to starve. After the war the white settlers became even bolder. In return for their contributions to the war effort, they demanded complete settler control of the colony, removing natives as they wished by whatever force was necessary. They instituted a registration system for all natives. To be without a registration card became a crime. The colonial government, under white settler influence, announced that the British crown owned the whole of Kenya and all native land agreements or arrangements were illegal.

Nairobi was the governing city of Kenya, the place where grievances could be aired, political rallies held, and petitions presented. The most prominent critic of the white land grab and the colonial government's support of it was a young man named Harry Thuku from a prominent and powerful Kikuyu family. He voiced Kikuyu grievances, criticized the government, and drew huge crowds. Within months the colonial government fired on a crowd at one of his speeches, arrested Thuku, and imprisoned him in the far south of Kenya. K. N. Johnstone was well aware of the imprisonment of Thuku and stayed clear of public involvement in politics. Though he was personally popular among Kikuyu in Nairobi, K. N. Johnstone did not participate in the founding of the first Kikuyu political organizations, formed in the early 1920s. These organizations mainly wrote petitions to the colonial government expressing their grievances.

From a global perspective, Kenya's pattern was typical of early resistance to colonialism and efforts to create an indigenous nationalism. In India, for example, petitions by a small group of educated elite men started thirty years earlier than they did in Kenya. As in Kenya, India had paid special taxes for the war effort and sent hundreds of thousands of men to fight; consequently, Indians felt that they should receive compensation and recognition from the colonial government. By the time petitions started in Kenya in the 1920s, a younger generation in India had already turned away from petitions to anticolonial mass movements and a nationalism that included self-rule. Gandhi and his message of nonviolent resistance and civil disobedience gained followers and momentum.

Around the world, resistance to colonial domination manifested similar patterns that were as much psychological as political. Colonialism included profound racism, which asserted that not only were colonized people permanently inferior to whites but also that they were incapable of self-rule. Indigenous nationalists went through periods of hope, when change seemed possible, followed by waves of betrayal and anger, when hopes were dashed. Radicalized by this process, some nationalists supported armed struggle; others advocated for taking power through local organizing; and still others in despair turned away from political organizing.

Kenyatta and London

By the mid-1920s a large Kikuyu organization known as the Kikuyu Central Association (KCA) needed a full-time spokesperson in Nairobi. The KCA approached K. N. Johnstone, who drove a hard bargain, demanding that they match his water department salary in addition to providing a housing allowance, a budget for supplies, and a motorcycle. The KCA accepted Johnstone's terms and signed a long-term contract with him in 1927. He traveled through Kikuyu lands with news of the colonial government and moves by white settlers. He drafted petitions and presented them to the government.[11]

In May of 1928 Johnstone produced the first issue of a newsletter for distribution to the Kikuyu members of his organization, though it is unlikely that he wrote the articles. The masthead included the slogan "Pray and Work," and the writing style was carefully diplomatic. The articles talked about progress for all communities in Kenya. One significant feature of this newsletter was the name of its secretary. Johnstone introduced himself to his new audience as Johnstone Kenyatta, suggesting his identification with all of Kenya, an unmistakable move toward nationalism. Johnstone remained part of his name to signal his mission background, Christianity, and connections with white society.[12]

Within the KCA, many felt that they would receive neither a proper hearing nor justice from Kenya's colonial government. The KCA leadership decided to send its own representative to London to marshal support for rolling back white land claims. Kenyatta agreed to go, and the KCA raised money for his passage, gave him letters of introduction, and promised to take care of his family. The colonial government made every effort to discourage his trip but could not prevent his departure. On May 17, 1929, Kenyatta boarded a French liner bound for England. Although he promised his wife to return to Kenya as soon as possible, Kenyatta would spend the next seventeen years in Europe.

The important point here is that a number of leading African and Asian nationalists learned about Western forms of nationalism by studying, traveling, and living in Europe and America. They read Voltaire in Paris or discussed Burke in London. They met people who sympathized with their desire for freedom and independence. Gandhi, Ho Chi Minh, and Kenyatta fit this pattern. Other Asian nationalists, however, did not spend time in Europe—for example, Mao Zedong (1893–1976), the Chinese communist revolutionary who became the founding father of the People's Republic of China. Modern scholarship on the development of nationalism outside Europe highlights several influences: local conditions and grievances, European writing on nationalism, and personal contacts with Europeans opposed to colonialism. These leaders realized that the same forms of colonial oppression were common practice in colonies, regardless of whether they were British, French, or American. Kenyatta may have known, for example, that confining First Nation populations to reservations was practiced in the United States just as it was in Kenya.

Like Ho Chi Minh, Kenyatta studied at a school for the colonized in Moscow. He was recruited by a Russian agent as a potential leader of a Marxist revolution in Africa. Worldwide revolution by the working class was taught as a truer, more lasting alternative to nationalism. A year later Stalin decided that Africans were too primitive to generate a proper Marxist revolution and closed the school. Kenyatta wrote that Marxism was just another means of keeping Africans down. He fled Russia and made his way back to England. For years he lived in a hostel that housed impoverished Christian, Muslim, and Hindu students adrift in London.

Looking Forward, Looking Back

In small anti-colonial British newspapers, Kenyatta wrote that his country could "advance" only though independence from Great Britain and representative self-rule. In this way Kenyatta's emerging nationalism looked forward, not back, and advocated for all people of Kenya to participate in its future. At the same time, Kenyatta studied at the London School of Economics with Branislaw Malinowski, one of the founders of modern anthropology. From this experience he wrote a book on the traditions and practices of the Kikuyu in the anthropological style of Malinowski and his students. Indeed, Malinowski wrote the introduction to the book, titled *Facing Mount Kenya* (1938).[13]

In the book Kenyatta describes Kikuyu myth, magic, and ritual. In the frontispiece picture, Kenyatta wears an animal skin cloak over one shoulder; the other shoulder remains bare. In one hand is a spear, the edge of which he fingers. Clearly the image is meant to link Kenyatta to his distant forebears. The book's author is "Jomo" Kenyatta, the result of brainstorming with a Kikuyu friend to find a more "African" name, which Kenyatta would keep for the rest of his life. The book lays out a golden age of the Kikuyu, before the coming of the Europeans; a time of prosperous connection to the land, accepted kinship patterns, leadership by

One of the stranger permutations of Kenyatta's shifting modes of dress was as an extra in the adventure film titled *Sanders of the River*, 1935. Much of it was shot in various locations in Africa. Paul Robeson starred in the film but disowned it for its open racism and colonialism.

the elders, family teaching of necessary skills, transmission of knowledge from generation to generation, and complementary roles for men and women. Kenyatta wanted true understanding of African life and language. He envisioned an educational system that would replace a Europe-centered curriculum with one that recognized the importance of African ways of thinking and living.

These two viewpoints, looking to the future and describing a golden past, might seem contradictory, but for nationalists they were not. Adjusting history to highlight a golden age was a regular feature of nationalist writing, whether in Europe or in colonies. The golden age offered a proven template of what the nation could achieve by itself. The golden age was conveniently long ago, long enough to preclude checking the facts. Nationalist histories downplayed ancient warfare between groups within the nation. Instead, they recounted the brave deeds of yore in repelling the foreign enemy. Nationalist programs, even those embracing radical social changes, could be portrayed as a return to the golden age.

War, Return, and Rebellion

When world war returned to Europe in 1939, Kenyatta's friends helped him leave London for the English countryside to avoid German bombing. The countryside also offered agricultural work, which made Kenyatta exempt from military service. Throughout the seven years of World War II in Europe (1939–1945) he worked as an agricultural laborer in Sussex, mainly in a hot house where he grew vegetables. He managed to rent a small house, plant a garden, and, despite his wife and family in Kenya, marry an English woman named Edna Clarke. He was occasionally able to attend meetings sponsored by younger Africans who were promoting pan-African unity. They advocated for the end to colonial dominance of individual countries but also for an association of new African nations to address common problems.

When the war ended in 1945, Kenyatta returned to promoting his view of the future of Kenya—a multiracial nation with education and opportunities for all. He left England, Edna, and their son behind, and arrived at Mombasa, Kenya's oldest and (after the capital Nairobi) largest city, in 1946. During his years in England the British colonial government of Kenya had appropriated from the tribes more than 10,000 square miles of prime agricultural land and granted it to the more than 30,000 white settlers. It was a very different Kenya to which Kenyatta returned.

Just as in World War I, Kenyans fought and died in World War II. These soldiers from Kenya had been stationed in a variety of countries and colonies. They met and conversed with soldiers from all parts of the world, hearing about racial discrimination in America and colonial oppression in India.[14] After the war native Kenyans agitated for civil rights, lower taxes, return of tribal land, and respect. Labor unions flourished despite the colonial government's attempts to suppress them. Secret societies grew. To his surprise Kenyatta was treated as a returning patriot and hero. He spoke at rallies and meetings as the elected head of the KCA and advocated a moderate plan: hard work, especially on the development of tribal land; an end to government corruption; and necessary unity among tribes. Nevertheless, the colonial government considered him a dangerous agitator and kept an open file on his activities.

An intransigent colonial government frustrated native Kenyan aspirations. The secret societies continued to expand, recruiting young men from both larger and smaller tribes. In clandestine, solemn rituals, new recruits swore to fight and die for the expulsion of the colonial government and freedom for the nation. Armed rebellion was discussed, though not publicly. Younger, more militant members of trade unions and tribes purged older, more moderate and

European settlers recruited "Home Guards" to fight against the Mau Mau "rebels." These same men may have fought for Britain during World War II.

cautious leaders. Police officers, government informants, and witnesses for court cases disappeared or were openly murdered.

In 1952, the secret societies broke into open rebellion against the white settlers and the colonial government. The Kikuyu were the principal fighters. What became known as the Mau Mau Rebellion was brutal, violent, and prolonged. Engaging in guerilla warfare, the fighters would strike and then retreat to jungle strongholds. They enjoyed considerable support in villages. As the rebellion dragged on through the 1950s, the colonial government adopted suppression tactics that had been developed in the British colony of Malaya. The army rounded up whole populations and confined them to resettlement camps. Without means to support themselves, the Kikuyu were forced to become wage labor on white settler farms. To attack the Kikuyu rebels and their supporters the colonial government recruited a large force (known as the Home Guard) from other tribes. The result was bloody intertribal and inter-religious warfare. Thirty thousand Kikuyu were rounded up in Nairobi and sent to resettlement camps. The border between Kikuyu country and the rest of Kenya was sealed.

From a global perspective, the Mau Mau Rebellion in Kenya was one of many guerilla anticolonial rebellions. In Vietnam, for example, Ho Chi Minh

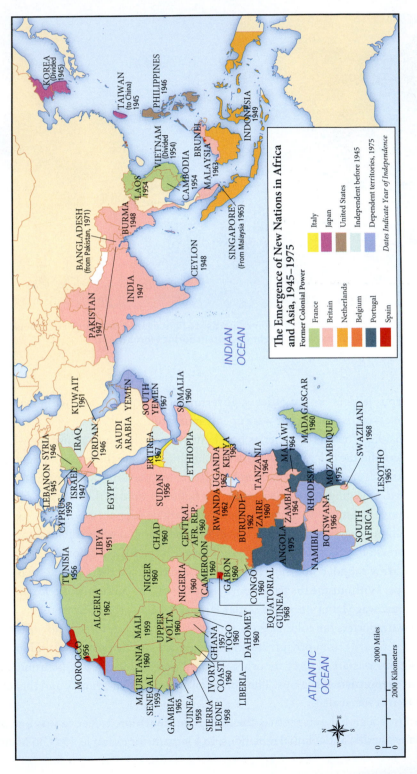

Map 2.3

The Emergence of New Nations in Africa and Asia, 1945–1975

Former Colonial Power

- France
- Britain
- Netherlands
- Belgium
- Portugal
- Spain
- Italy
- Japan
- United States
- Independent before 1945
- Dependent territories, 1975

Dates Indicate Year of Independence

led decades-long guerilla warfare against the French, and later the Americans. Jewish settlers in Palestine waged the same sort of guerilla warfare against the British colonial government. Colonial governments everywhere treated armed rebellion as a "public order" problem and military suppression as the solution. When freedom was finally achieved, its close association with violent resistance was a deep and abiding legacy.

Even though Kenyatta had spoken repeatedly against the Mau Mau and their tactics, the colonial government believed he was the secret mastermind of the rebellion, arrested him in 1952, and sentenced him to prison for life. By 1960, the British government made it clear that it was moving rapidly to freedom and self-rule on a "one-man, one-vote" basis. The white settlers would get no special representation. Various native political organizations demanded Kenyatta's release before serious negotiations could begin.

Kenyatta finally left prison in 1961. Both the colonial government and the white press had portrayed him as responsible for Mau Mau violence. This publicity made him a hero, and massive crowds welcomed him along his route home. When freedom finally did come, in June 1963, Kenyatta served as Kenya's first prime minister. Basic problems of nationalism remained.[15] Were white settlers part of the new nation? What was to be done about the thousands of Indians in crucial positions in government and in business? Were they part of the nation or not? How did commitment to the nation differ from loyalty to the tribe?[16] What events of Kenya's past were to be forgotten, and what events were to be foregrounded?[17] Did nationalism include close and significant ties to other new nations in East Africa? What about violence as a political strategy? These issues would play out in politics and in the streets for decades after Kenya's independence.[18]

The Bigger Picture

Nationalism and Its Challenges

As the American historian Hayden White elegantly formulated decades ago, nationalism is an "imagined community," a belief system, and can be challenged only by another belief system.[19] Believers advocate and work for their ideals and hope to bring specific aspects of the nation into reality. In this way nationalism was (and is) like an ordering of society based on the demands and laws of a divine entity. Believing in the nation was (and is) just as emotional an experience as religious faith and worship.

Participation in the nation seems so normal, so matter-of-fact, that it almost disappears. People pay taxes to support the nation. Cars travel national highways. Tourists visit national parks, battlefields, and museums. National holidays come and go, some with fireworks, others with church services. Schoolchildren study the formation of the nation. Government agencies focus on national security, national health, national energy policy, and nationally controlled bandwidth. Passports and visas are usually required to cross national borders. The United Nations and the Olympics embody the idea that nations are the proper way to divide up the earth's continents. When it seems to work, few pay attention. In India, for example, the national anthem is played before every movie. Everyone stands and sings along. Local people, who have performed this ritual all their lives, barely notice the anthem and its singing.

One scholar has termed this day-to-day process "banal nationalism," which subtly reinforces loyalty to the nation in acts embedded in common events. The nation remains a source of meaning, comfort, and fellow feeling in the modern world, what British historian Benedict Anderson terms "confidence in a solid community moving steadily up (or down) history."[20] Nationalism is a deep belief within citizens and is tapped in small ways daily. Predictions that nationalism would disappear in the face of economic globalization and large-scale migrations have proved wrong. If anything, both globalization and migration have provoked nationalism in a host of countries across the world.

Waving Spanish flags, members of the hyper-nationalist Vox Party take to the streets in 2018.

Internal or external political events, however, can rapidly turn banal nationalism into charged debates over unresolved aspects of the nation: Who are we? Who do we stand with or against? Why do we fight? What should our children be taught, and in what language? These and other debates shift the very terms with which nationalism is discussed. If a country at one moment considers shared language its main basis of nationalism, sometime later the emphasis might shift to demonizing an enemy country with an objectionable ideology. Nationalism's accentuation of one ethnicity is little removed from violent ethnic cleansing of minorities. Nationalism's ideal of a single shared religion has led to religious persecution and outright pogroms. Religious persecution as part of nationalism has played out in, for example, anti-Muslim violence in India, Myanmar, and China and anti-Christian violence in Pakistan, Iraq, and Egypt. The ideal of a shared, common history has resulted in denigration, even vilification, of those outside of or opposed to the featured events of the national history. Nationalism's single-race ideal opens the way for racism. Hard national boundaries can make enemies of neighbors. Nationalism has a long and bloody history as the justification for violence. A nation championed as strong may be unjust, cruel, undemocratic, or thoroughly oppressive of women and minorities.[21]

It must be understood that nationalism is an ongoing process. Just as nationalism brought people together into states, so the same ideology can shatter states with considerable violence, as when Pakistan was split off from India in 1947 and when Bangladesh gained independence from Pakistan in 1971. Also in the past half-century or so a single Korea divided into North and South. Vietnam became two countries only later to reunite. Yugoslavia broke up into seven nations. The Soviet Union divided into fifteen nations. Eretria broke free from Ethiopia. East and West Germany reunified. Scotland and Quebec held secessionist referenda, though both failed. Independence movements are a continuing feature of states and peoples across the world, including the Philippines, India, many states in Africa, the Basques in Spain and France, the Kurds in Turkey and Iraq, and indigenous people in Central and South America. Twenty-eight nations joined the European Union; Britain has recently left it.

Nationalism matters because the loyalty it demands has affected life and death in the starkest possible terms. When US President George H. W. Bush spoke of the necessity of the Gulf War in January 1991, he justified it largely on the basis of nations and nationalism. Iraq leader Saddam Hussein had invaded the nation of Kuwait and attempted to absorb it into the nation of Iraq. Bush announced that Iraq's invasion demanded war because "no nation will be permitted to brutally assault its neighbor." Invading a nation with the intent of extinguishing it was about the worst, most barbaric thing a nation could do. Americans took up the call to battle, as did many other nations (eventually called "the Coalition"), and quickly drove the Iraq forces out of Kuwait.

Though the Gulf War was recognized as a decisive victory for the Coalition, Kuwait and Iraq suffered enormous damage, and Saddam Hussein remained in power.

Each generation must form its own nationalism. The ongoing danger is the substitution of emotional nationalism for rational discussion of policy and the shutting down of opposition as enemies of the nation.[22] Perhaps it is best to treat the nation as a process—an unfinished, incomplete dialogue. In considering the various calls for loyalty and commitment, we need to stay vigilant and skeptical of what is suggested in the name of the nation. Why are some wars featured and others left out of national histories?[23] Does the story of the nation include violence against religious minorities? What presence do women have in the story of the nation? How do minorities figure in the

TIMELINE

ca. 300 CE
Kikuyu begin to live in the area around Mount Kenya

1869
First rail line across the United States

1884–1885
Berlin conference carves up Africa among European powers

1895
British colonial government lays the first rails inland from the port of Mombasa

ca. 1897
Jomo Kenyatta is born

1914
Kenyatta leaves Christian evangelist mission

1927
Kenyatta (then going by K. N. Johnstone) becomes spokesperson of the Kikuya Central Association (KCA) in Nairobi

1928
First newsletter for KCA is published by Kenyatta

1929
Kenyatta leaves for Europe, studies at the London School of Economics and advocates for the independence of Kenya

1938
Kenyatta publishes *Facing Mount Kenya*

1946
Kenyatta leaves Europe for Mombasa

nation? How is nature treated by the nation? Is it an inexhaustible resource or a finite and precious one? Only by interrogating what is said and done in the name of the nation can we find suitable responses to these and other questions that will shape the future.

For digital learning resources, please go to
www.oup.com/he/gordon-seventhemes1e

1952
Mau Mau break into open rebellion against white settlers and the colonial government

1952
Kenyatta is arrested and sentenced to prison for life, accused of being the mastermind behind the rebellion

1960
British colonial government in Kenya moves to freedom and self-rule on "one man-one vote" basis

1961
Kenyatta is released from prison

1963
Kenya gains independence from Great Britain

1963
Kenyatta becomes Kenya's first prime minister

Technology and Science

The Example of Glass

The Big Picture: What Is Technology?

When we talk of technology, it seems obvious what we are talking about: tools and machines such as solar panels, computers, cell phones, and 3-D printers. The definition of technology is more complicated than it seems. Adam Thierer, author of the blog *The Technology Liberation Front*, compiled a list of twenty different definitions of technology. The Merriam-Webster dictionary keeps it short but vague, defining technology as the "practical application of knowledge especially in a particular area" (as in "medical technology"). More thorough definitions in the literature on technology emphasize the organization of *scientific* knowledge to achieve a practical end. Think of how the scientific knowledge of the expansion of water when it is heated is applied to a closed cylinder that rotates a shaft—the steam engine. This chapter defines significant new technology as an invention that either directly changes society or produces something that affects survival, health, material well-being, or values and beliefs.

> View of the stained-glass windows of Sainte-Chapelle, a royal chapel built in the thirteenth century, Paris, France.

Such a definition suggests the themes and questions central to this chapter. Was technology a central driver of major changes in how people lived, spent their time, found work, sustained social relationships, and thought of themselves and others? Did it create new money-making opportunities, increase geographic mobility, and significantly alter the size and functioning of organizations? Was there a single "scientific method" by which men and women discovered and tested new technology?

We will also consider the possibility that new technology did not significantly drive history but was instead fragile, and frequently failed. Did it require special materials not locally available? What were the limitations on transport? Did existing processes compete with the new technology and hinder its adoption? Were there crucial trade secrets, passed only through teacher-student relations in families, guilds, or castes? How much capital did an entrepreneur have to commit to begin making the new invention?

Of the thousands of technological changes through human history this chapter tells the story of one: glass. Though glass seems prosaic today, the stuff of storm windows, beer steins, and automobile headlights, glass in the ancient world was a mysterious material, solid but transparent, radiant in sunlight, opaque in shadow, and smooth to the touch. It was imbued with spiritual and magical power.

Three features of glass make it valuable to study as a technology. First, the processes of glassmaking date from antiquity. Artisans made glass objects 4,000 years ago in Egypt and the Middle East and slightly later in India and China. Second, early glass technology did not spread to the rest of the ancient world—not to Africa, Central Asia, the Americas, or other regions. Third, the historical record allows us to test whether glassmaking technology actually affected the survival, health, material well-being, and values of the surrounding society.

The creation of glass followed a long process of trial and error. Melting sand (silicon dioxide) at 1,700 to 2,100 degrees Fahrenheit yields a material with looser chemical bonds, which we know as glass. The ancient world, however, could not produce the high temperatures necessary to make glass. Relentless experimentation revealed that the ash derived by the burning of a few plants lowered the melt temperature, but the resulting glass was fragile and brittle. The addition of seashells stabilized the glass. Then ancient craftsmen learned that the mixture of sand, ash, and seashells had to be finely ground and carefully roasted ahead of melting. Colored glass required small amounts of a ground metal oxide. Cobalt oxide produced a deep blue, and copper oxide produced red. These oxides came from a tiny number of mines and were shipped across the ancient Middle East.

Craftsmen had to search out and experiment with local sand or beach pebbles, supplement them with local seashells or other sources of calcium, figure out their own techniques of raising the kiln temperature, and test their own mineral ores as colorants. It is easy to imagine failures in hundreds upon hundreds of locations.

Over millennia, only three centers were able to overcome the obstacles to glassmaking and to sustain it as a viable craft. The first was the eastern Mediterranean, what is today Egypt, Israel, Syria, and Iraq. Farther east, glassmaking in India was an indigenous invention (perhaps ca. 1200 BCE). Modern chemical analysis has shown that the composition of early Indian glass was distinctly different from the glass made in the eastern Mediterranean. The third indigenous development of glass was around 1000 BCE in China.[1] The formula for Chinese glass contained lead and barium, which melted at a low temperature but yielded only frail glass. After centuries, some Chinese artisans shifted to a more stable glass formula, probably under the influence of foreign makers.

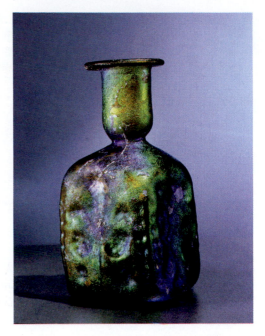

Late Roman amber glass jar, ca. 284–500 CE.

Craftsmen in the ancient world produced glass mainly as a cheaper alternate to already coveted natural materials. In Egypt, colored glass amulets and jewelry substituted for extremely expensive lapis lazuli from Afghanistan and turquoise from Iran. In China, glass beads and disks with embedded darker streaks mimicked the expensive jade used in ritual and burial objects. In India, colored glass bangles were the affordable alternative to gold or silver bangles. In Rome, glass dishes, cups, bowls, and platters became the middle-class alternative to the elite's costly vessels of carved rock crystal.

It is important to note the limitations on technological innovation and adoption, however. First, there was nothing inevitable about the discovery of the technology of glassmaking. Though it was independently developed in the eastern Mediterranean, India, and China, glassmaking was never invented in the pre-Columbian Americas, despite of the great sophistication of many ancient American cultures in the parallel field of ceramics. Second, the knowledge required for glassmaking was limited and transitory. Glassmaking technology spread to new sites, but it also could also be lost. The mixture of metallic oxides and kiln conditions that produced a distinctive color was usually a family secret and often disappeared, never to be duplicated. After the collapse of the western Roman Empire, glassmaking secrets were lost and the craft basically disappeared from Europe for 700 years. Third, the discovery of glassmaking technology did

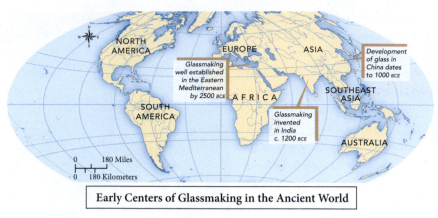

Map 3.1

Early Centers of Glassmaking in the Ancient World

not necessarily spur further technological progress in the field. India, for example, made only beads and bangles in 1000 BCE and continued to do so for more than 2,000 years.

Overall, glassmaking technology does not seem to have made all that much difference in the ancient world. It did not fundamentally change how people lived, saw themselves and others, found work, sustained social relationships, or went to war. Ancient technology seems to have proceeded over long periods of incremental change.

Modern technology, by contrast, seems driven by the goals to save time and enhance well-being and convenience. Industrial and research groups compete to be the first to bring a new technology to market. We know the names of inventors of breakthrough technology, where the work was done, and who were the colleagues involved. (Even the idea of "breakthrough" seems unlikely in the ancient world.) The remainder of the chapter will track the shift from ancient glassmaking to glass as a modern technology. Our story begins in ninth-century CE Baghdad.

Lenses in Theory and Practice

In the ninth century the centrality and importance of glass began to change. Caliph Harun al-Rashid of Baghdad, ruler of the Muslim world, began an extraordinary and audacious project, nothing less than the gathering of all the wisdom of the known world. He hired men to locate and purchase learned texts and paid translators to render them from Greek, Assyrian, Hebrew, Persian, and Sanskrit into Arabic. Subsequent caliphs recruited philosophers and doctors, mathematicians and astronomers, and geographers and botanists from as far away as India. These learned men met and worked in a palace purposely-built for them. It was known as the House of Wisdom.

Among this august company was an Arab scientist, philosopher, and mathematician named Abu Ali al-Hasan ibn al-Haytham (965–1040 CE). In the

West he is known as Alhazen, a Latinized form of his Arabic first name, al-Hasan. He wrote a seven-volume compendium on optics, how light works. It was much more than a summary of what was known. Alhazen formulated experiments to prove or disprove prior theories of the nature of light and how it interacted with various materials.

Frontispiece to the first printed Latin translation of Alhazen's *Book of Optics*. The image shows several of the optical phenomena examined by Alhazen, including the use of mirrors to concentrate sunlight to destroy ships.

Advances in Lens Technology

As we have seen, in Europe glassmaking almost entirely disappeared after the end of the western Roman Empire. When glassmaking returned to Europe in the twelfth century, Alhazen provided the theoretical framework and practical suggestions for crafting sophisticated lenses. Over centuries Dutch eyeglass makers became steadily more adept at grinding lenses to compensate for various failings of the human eye, especially nearsightedness. (Just as in the ancient Middle East and China, glass technology once again adapted to an existing demand.) For their wealthy customers, eyeglass producers demanded more optical purity from glassmakers. By the seventeenth century glassworks had spread throughout Europe. Bohemian glass, for example, competed with glass from Strasbourg and Saxony in Germany, Vienna, Paris, and Venice. The demand seemed insatiable among the wealthy for high-quality eyeglasses and crystal-clear glass plates, cups, and platters.[2]

Two Dutchmen, Jacob Metius and Hans Lippershey, are credited with combining a convex lens (to spread light) and a concave lens (to concentrate light) into what was termed a "far-seeing" device on its debut in 1608. It was made famous, however, by the Italian astronomer and physicist Galileo Galilei (1564–1642), who—never having seen the Dutch devices—constructed his own telescope from lenses available in his home city of Venice. He steadily improved his telescopes and was the first to turn a telescope toward the stars, discovering four satellites of Jupiter and assembling evidence that the stars and the planets, including earth, revolved around the sun, upending the view accepted since antiquity that earth was the center of the universe.

European Glassmaking Centers, ca. 1600

North Sea · Baltic Sea · ATLANTIC OCEAN · Mediterranean Sea

ENGLAND · London · Delft · LOW COUNTRIES · GERMANY · SAXONY · Liège · Prague · BOHEMIA · Paris · Strasbourg · Vienna · Bourges · FRANCE · Lyon · Murano · Venice · Florence · ITALY

0 — 250 Miles
0 — 250 Kilometers

Map 3.2

Galileo's findings provoked intense debates about nature, the larger universe, and the relationship between theology and science. Was truth discovered by observation of the natural world and application of human reason, or was truth found in holy scripture and religious texts? The Catholic Inquisition convicted Galileo of heresy and forced him to recant his celestial findings. The Church could not, however, contain a century of improvements in lenses and a frenzy of lens-based scientific research. The lenses provided the data for scientists and philosophers to debate the very meaning of truth and human beings' place in the universe.

Leeuwenhoek's Observations

Our guide to this period of intense lens-based research is Antony van Leeuwenhoek (1632–1723), a Dutch cloth merchant and minor official who spent his whole life in the small city of Delft in Holland. Until 1674, when Leeuwenhoek was forty-two years old, scholars know only the bureaucratic facts of his life—birth, marriage, death of his mother, purchase of a house, birth of his children, death of his first wife, second marriage, and appointment to government posts. None of this suggests that he was more than a solid middle-class citizen of Delft. How utterly wrong is this assessment. Through his newly developed microscope he had the rare pleasure of seeing things that no human had ever seen before.

Leeuwenhoek was tenacious, inventive, and endlessly curious. In 1674, a local Delft doctor recommended his findings to the Royal Society in England. Leeuwenhoek had already studied plants and animals around him for years, and the good doctor knew the basis for the cloth merchant's acute observations:[3]

> I am writing to tell you that a certain most ingenious person here named Leewenhoek [a name spelled various ways by different sources] has devised microscopes which far surpass those which we have hitherto seen. . . . the enclosed letter from him, wherein he describes certain things which he has observed more accurately than previous authors, will afford you a sample of his work:[4]

Leeuwenhoek's accompanying letter lays out his misgivings about entering the larger scientific world of the time:

> I have oft-times been besought by divers gentlemen, to set down on paper what I have beheld through my newly invented *Microscopi*; but I have generally declined; first because I have no style or pen, wherewith to express my thoughts properly; secondly, because I have not been brought up to languages or arts, but only to business; and in the third place, because I do not suffer contradiction or censure from others.[5]

This unpromising beginning blossomed into a fifty-year string of letters and responses between Leeuwenhoek and members of the Royal Society, which ceased only at his death. He wrote in Dutch (the only language he knew), but the observations were so treasured that the Society routinely had them translated into either Latin or English and published in its scientific journal, *Philosophical Transactions*.

In May, June, and July of 1675 (a year after his initial letter to the Royal Society), Leeuwenhoek observed ordinary rain and well water through his microscope and found them teeming with life: "Little animals were, to my eye, more than ten thousand times smaller than the animalculs which Swammerdam has portrayed, and called Water-fleas or water-louse, which you can see alive and moving in water with the bare eye."[6] The letter described tiny organisms that ate, swam, and reproduced. Some moved by flexing filaments covering the body (now known as "ciliates"). Others used a whip-like tail to propel themselves (now termed "flagellates"). Still others moved by rotation (now known as "rotifers"). In this series of observations Leeuwenhoek also described bacteria, much the smallest living thing seen to that point in human history.[7] He found a world of tiny plant structures. Wood was not merely wood but a

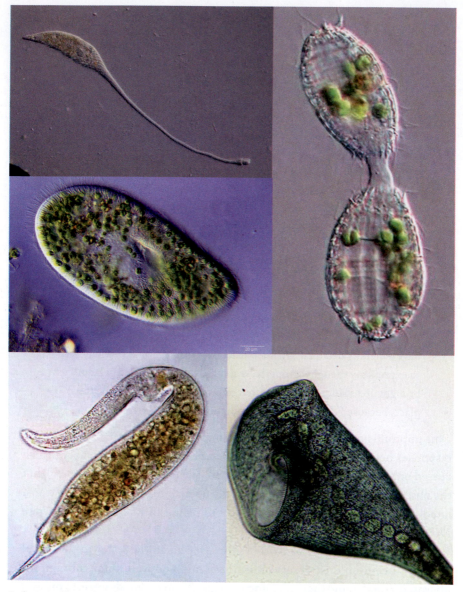

A photo collage showing a group of ciliates commonly found in water, much like the ones Leeuwenhoek observed through his microscope.

dizzyingly complex substance of various elements and purposes. Blood was not merely a liquid but had many components of different shapes and sizes.

These observations were at approximately 256x magnification (meaning 256 times larger than actual), which required extremely pure, optically clear glass without any impurities and tough enough to be ground. Such glass was available but not common.[8] Leeuwenhoek's lenses were tiny, no bigger than

A microscope designed and built by Leeuwenhoek around 1700. The specimen was placed on a pin manipulated by two sets of screws.

the nail of a little finger.[9] Some scholars have speculated that Leeuwenhoek invented and built his own lens-grinding machine. A more creative but equally plausible suggestion is that he dipped a steel rod into a pot of molten glass, removed the rod from the pot, and held it vertically so that a drip formed on the end of the rod. After the drip cooled, Leeuwenhoek snapped it off the rod and ground the broken join flat. But this is conjecture. Nowhere in his vast correspondence does Leeuwenhoek reveal his lens-making secrets.[10]

Consider what exactly was the "technology" involved in these breakthroughs. Was it the method and equipment of production of optically pure glass? Was it Leeuwenhoek's actual process of crafting lenses? Was it the mental process of converting drawings, notes, and speculation into actual lenses?

Leeuwenhoek and the Scientific Method

Scholars agree that Leeuwenhoek was an early practitioner of the scientific method while disagreeing on the definition of the term. Researchers, for example, vigorously debate whether different scientific methods define different disciplines. Equally vigorous debate surrounds whether scientific method demands reproducible results or must include prediction.

There is consensus, however, over the meaning of "method" in "scientific method." Method includes both understanding and doing. The scientific method begins with observation. Noting the features of the environment is the critical first step. Curiosity was central to Leeuwenhoek's method. He wanted to know about the microstructure of everything around him, from the cell structure of trees to the composition of human blood. Many formulations of scientific method then require the researcher to condense his or her general observations of, say, a bird wing to an answerable question. For example, how do the feathers stay in a certain pattern rather than getting tangled up?

At this point, formulations of scientific method diverge. Does the question need to be further condensed to a testable hypothesis or claim? (For example, feathers have special structures that repair small tangles.) What evidence will support this claim? How much effort should be spent in controlling all parameters outside the one being tested? Is numerical data the only valid data? How will the researcher connect analysis of the evidence to support the claim? As practiced by researchers, scientific method varies, for example, between a psychologist and a chemist. Working researchers, however, emphasize three components of their work rarely featured in the literature on scientific method. The first is the importance of a community of researchers, all working on similar observations or problems. Second, contacts with individuals outside that community are vital. They might be working on an overlapping problem or approaching the same problem in a different way. Scholarly conferences and publications are critical in this process. The third feature cited by working researchers is history, particularly the history of attempts to understand and solve a problem. Patent searches, for example, often show what did not work, which is crucial information for a researcher.

And how does Leeuwenhoek measure up on this broad view of scientific method? Actually, quite well. Let us take as an example his observations of crosscut sections of oak trees. He first observed the sheer number and variety of microscopic tubes, which he correctly assumed carried liquids up and down the tree. He then connected the structure and density of tree tubes to climate. The tubes were smaller in oak trees from colder, slower-growing regions. By closely examining growth rings he also connected the larger tubes with spring seasonal growth. His hypothesis was that because oak from very cold climates had fewer large tubes with thick walls, the overall wood would be weaker. He attempted to bolster this hypothesis with anecdotal data on oak grown in England and France versus oak cut in the Scandinavian countries. Leeuwenhoek recognized that—if he was right—the relative strengths of oak had important implications for the building industry and shipbuilding. He presented his findings to the Royal Society as a community that treasured both interesting scientific findings and welcomed practical and economic implications of the findings. Leeuwenhoek had no facilities to test the relative strength of Scandinavian versus English oak, so he could not collect data to prove his hypothesis. (Incidentally, Leeuwenhoek was wrong. Slow-growing, tightly grained oak is generally stronger than more rapidly growing oak.)

Lenses and Realism: Photography

By 1800 inventors had worked out many of the problems of lenses, such as blurriness apart from the center of the image and prism effects, which cast sharp edges into fuzzy colors. One crucial piece of scientific observation, however, remained unsolved. No simple and compelling way existed for researchers to record what they saw and to present their findings to their peers and the public. No single breakthrough solved this problem. Instead, across Europe hundreds of researchers went to work, generally presenting their results at meetings of scientific societies.

At one such conference, an amateur experimenter in France announced his discovery that silver iodide turned black in bright sunlight, yielding an image in places shielded from the sun. The race for photography was on. Researchers experimented with every phase of the process, such as exposing other chemicals to sunlight, creating various chemical solutions to hold silver nitrate onto a flat surface, making images on different substrates (pewter, tin, glass), and figuring out how to "fix" the image chemically so that it did not further darken when exposed to in ordinary light. New methods, materials, and processes steadily reduced the time required to make an image from hours to minutes. The size, weight, and cost of equipment to make photographs dropped dramatically.

Entrepreneurs saw opportunities beyond the scientific uses for photography. Painters bemoaned the "end of art," fearing that photographs would replace their portraits at a fraction of the cost. They were only partly right. Photographers did take pictures of wealthy families in studios. Wealthy people, however, still wanted portraits. The craft of the artist was to control lighting and contrast to improve the chin, eyes, or nose.

Photography met the desire of ordinary people for a visual record of their family through the years: husbands and wives, children, and family gatherings. By the mid-nineteenth century itinerant photographers traveled rural North America and rural Europe, setting up their cumbersome apparatus in small towns and villages.

In a pattern dating back millennia, a new technology offered something almost as good as the "real thing" at a lower price. The wealthy in ancient China owned costly jade ritual objects, and the wealthy in the Roman Empire ate off expensive carved rock crystal. The less wealthy in China replaced jade with glass that looked like jade, and less wealthy Romans ate off glass plates rather than rock crystal.

An ancient Egyptian temple in Luxor, Egypt, photographed by Frank Mason Good around 1860. With its rich history and stunning antiquities, Egypt was a favorite destination for early travel photographers.

Adding together the effects of lenses on scientific exploration and photography's images, it is difficult to overstate the importance of optically clear lenses as a new technology in the modern world. The new images of the tiny, the vast, and the familiar raised a host of questions. How did photographs affect one's self-image or image of others? How did photos affect notions of family, gender, work, and leisure? Why were stereo photos of faraway places—Egypt, China, Africa, India, Southeast Asia—so wildly popular in the West as parlor recreation in the last decades of the nineteenth century? Was it seeing someone or something thrillingly exotic without the difficulties or expense of foreign travel?

Flat Glass: Light and Reflection

Equally rich for understanding technology is the history of flat glass, which also had dramatic effects on how people lived, worked, and thought about themselves. At the time of Leeuwenhoek there were only three methods for making flat glass for windows and mirrors. One method, termed "crown glass," began with a small ball of hot glass on the end of a blowpipe. A craftsman (the "blower") blew a bubble inside the ball while steadily rotating it to keep the ball regular on all sides. After reheating, the blower blew further to turn the small ball of glass into a large one. Immediately, a helper pierced the bubble opposite the blowpipe and opened the ball to a disk, while the blower rotated the developing disk to keep it as regular and flat as possible. The helper removed the completed disk from the blowpipe and moved it to an annealing oven (an oven for heating and gradually cooling glass to render it less brittle). Three intrinsic problems limited this process. No matter how skilled the blower and his assistant, spinning the disk resulted in glass very thick toward the center (where the blowglass connected to the ball) to quite thin at the outer edge. Rotating the disk also produced waves and ridges, which could not be removed. Impurities in local materials generally yielded greenish or brownish glass, not true clear glass. The disk was therefore always cut into small pieces, which—if the job demanded some uniformity—could be matched to sections cut from other disks. Meanwhile, the thick center section of the disk was often sold off cheaply as low-grade glass.

The second method of making flat glass was known as "cylinder glass." Our guide to this process is a man named Albert Noe, who made cylinder glass in small factories in southern Ohio in the mid-twentieth century.[11] He was interviewed in 1975, shortly after his retirement, and gave us a firsthand detailed

"Flashing out" to form a circular sheet of glass. Nineteenth century.

description of the process.[12] Cylinder glass required a furnace on a platform about fifteen feet above the floor and five highly skilled artisans. The "gatherer" and the "blower" were located on the high platform. To begin a sheet of glass, the gatherer plunged a steel blowpipe into a pot of molten glass and drew out a ball on the end of the pipe, which he (rarely a "she") quickly passed to the blower. The blower was generally "a huge man, big, barrel chested." He blew an air bubble into the ball of molten glass and returned the pipe to the gatherer to add more glass, eventually resulting in a sphere of thirty pounds or more. The blower next lowered this sphere—still attached to the blowpipe—over the edge of the platform and swung it back and forth in an arc. This action stretched the sphere into a cylinder "6 to 8 feet long" and "18 to 20 inches across," which required blowing, continuous rotation, and great skill to keep the walls of the cylinder regular. Noe tells us, "Of course the longer the cylinder, the thinner the glass." This stage had to be done quickly, before the glass cooled and set. Meanwhile the gatherer ran off the platform and, stationed at ground level, used a cold piece of wood or steel to snap off the bottom of the cylinder and—while a heavily gloved assistant held the cylinder—sever the connection to the blowpipe. Noe remembers the gatherers as "very adept. I used to marvel at them. . . . It would fracture [snaps his fingers], just like that." As Noe explains, the cylinder cooled a bit, then was transported to the "flattening" room, where a skilled worker ran a hot rod down the length of the cylinder and touched the heated area with a piece of cold steel. The cylinder would split lengthwise. The split cylinder was then placed in an annealing oven at just the right temperature to "relax" and open gradually to a flat piece. Workers used water-soaked oak boards to flatten the glass. Noe says, "It was terrible quality glass, bowed, and we never were able to flatten it out completely." When the glass sheet was cool, a "cutter" cut around thin spots, bubbles, and embedded impurities. Albert Noe was the son of a cutter, and three of his brothers were in the same trade.

And how did Albert Noe, his brothers, and his father end up as skilled glass craftsmen in southern Ohio? The answer is simple. In a pattern dating back to the Middle Ages, the way to transfer technology was to relocate the people who knew the process. In Noe's father's generation, US entrepreneurs recruited hundreds of experienced glassworkers from Belgium and France. These workers formed strong unions, required three-year apprenticeships, and made it almost impossible for anyone but a family member to join. As Noe says, this was the way most flat glass was produced in the United States until 1928, when a machine to produce glass cylinders was introduced.[13]

Flat glass production did, however, have one third method, termed "plate glass." French king Louis XIV (r. 1643–1715), the absolutist ruler who coined the phrase "l'etat, c'est moi" ("the state, it is I"), wanted brighter mirrors and larger windows for the Palace of Versailles, his royal residence and center of government. He gathered the top French glassmaking talent at the village of Saint-Gobain, sixty miles northeast of Paris, and chartered the glassworks as a royal workshop. In 1687 one of the glassmakers at Saint-Gobain invented a wholly new glassmaking technology. Workers dipped a large iron ladle into a crucible of molten glass and poured the glass onto an iron table. Then craftsmen paddled the glass relatively flat and moved the table under a set of large steel rollers, which thinned and spread the glass into a sheet. While the glass was still hot, workers trimmed the sheet, cut out sections with air bubbles, cut it into big rectangular panels, and moved it to an annealing oven. Large overhead machines ground and polished the faces and edges of each sheet. The process was slow, laborious, and expensive, but it produced optically flat, smooth, and clear sheets of large size.

The limitations on the spread of this new technique were formidable. The capital investment to duplicate the French royal glassworks was very high, as were the risks. The new plate glass was thick (as much as an inch), and the large sheets often cracked from internal stress. No one was convinced of demand for large panes of glass outside of a few royal palaces. About a century after the invention of plate glass in France, however, a few glassworks in England began to make it and through many small improvements beat the French in quality and in price.[14]

In Europe and the United States, the demand for large-scale flat glass moved beyond palaces to fashionable restaurants. Tall mirrors became the hallmark of the locales where the wealthy looked at themselves and one another. Demand for superior flat glass for windows also came from urban shopkeepers, especially owners of high-end stores. Strolling the streets of these fashionable shops alerted city-dwellers to what was in style season-by-season. Window-shopping was born. By the mid-nineteenth century, general goods stores even in provincial towns displayed the new national brands of soap, skin lotions, and toothpaste behind plate glass windows at the front of the store.

Confronted with the high price of imported plate glass, shops and restaurants in the United States still wanted fashionable show windows and mirrors. The first efforts of US glassworks to make plate glass date from the early 1850s. In the following three decades every US attempt to make plate glass ended in financial failure. The glass was so expensive and the failure rate so high that, as a modern glass historian puts it, "Despite considerable efforts on the part of glassmakers, entrepreneurs, and investors alike, until 1880 not a single piece of plate glass was made in America without loss to the manufacturer, and all funds invested in the enterprise had vanished without result."[15]

Once again, we see that technology did not rush to the rescue. Despite proven demand and masses of capital investment, the glassmaking industry in the United States could not make flat, bubble-free, clear glass until 1880, after decades of trying. The two US companies that eventually succeeded in making affordable, high-quality flat glass—Libbey-Owens-Ford and Pittsburgh Plate Glass—imported the technology and the workers from Europe and invested far more capital than had earlier attempts.

Flat Glass: The Success Story

The production of large flat glass finally became industrial and largely automated in the 1930s. In this new process, the various components of glass were finely ground and fed continuously into a large furnace. Molten glass exited the furnace in the form of a thick ribbon, which was gradually shaped by steel rollers. When the ribbon of glass was cool, machines ground and polished both sides and edges.

The new continuous plate glass was far less expensive than earlier processes. It became an integral part of the new tall buildings at the center of cities. By the opening decades of the twentieth century, entrepreneurs built glass into skyscrapers in New York, Philadelphia, Boston, Chicago, St. Louis, Cleveland, and Cincinnati. Height restrictions and concerns for safety limited skyscraper development in Europe, although a few appeared in Holland, Germany, and England. These new buildings—office towers, hotels, and department stores—redefined office work, elegant travel, and urban shopping. They required vast amounts of flat glass for large windows and lobby mirrors. Makers of flat glass, notably Libbey-Owens-Ford and Pittsburgh Plate Glass, met this demand and by the 1950s provided 96 percent of the flat glass sold in the United States.[16]

Today's flat glass is made by a process invented in the 1950s termed "float glass." The glass exits the furnace literally floating on a ribbon of liquid tin, which is so dense that the glass does not stick to it. The ribbon of glass gradually cools, both faces becoming optically clear, with no grinding necessary. The only drawback of the process is the very high capital cost—more than 150 million dollars for a new plant. Six companies produce virtually all of the flat glass manufactured worldwide. Nevertheless, flat glass became optically clear, predictable, reliable, and inexpensive. Glass-clad skyscrapers became cost effective and common. Home designs featured larger windows and more of them. Storm windows kept out the cold. Sliding glass doors connected the inside and the outside. National housekeeping and design magazines promoted indoor-outdoor patio living.

The large openings in the framework of the Empire State building (1931) were divided to match available window glass.

The Bigger Picture

Evaluating New Technology

Our exploration of glassmaking invites us to reconsider the various definitions of technology. First, definitions that limit technology to the application of modern *scientific* knowledge to practical problems shortchange the processes and uses of technology in the ancient world. The technologies to raise water for irrigation, to move heavy blocks of stone across the landscape, or to create fired and glazed pots were all solutions to practical problems, but none of them were discovered by the scientific method. Whoever devised local solutions to local problems was surely illiterate, but no less a creator of important technology. Second, definitions that limit technology to material objects (a steam engine or a light bulb, for example) are too narrow: the process of thinking about some better method seems to have always been an inseparable part of breakthrough technology. Third, the question of why a technology appeared at a particular time and place is key. Definitions that reduce the appearance of a technology to a universal drive for efficiency or a better life for the beneficiaries of the technology miss just how complex was new technology's actual relation to the surrounding society.

Did glassmaking participate in an Industrial Revolution? In briefest summary, the standard description of the nineteenth-century Industrial Revolution centers on re-placement of highly skilled craftsmen in small workshops by production in new, large factories that ran sophisticated and accurate machines. Unlike a craft shop, output depended on repetitive movements by single-function machines, which required less skilled workers than the artisans of craft shops. The result was that factories sold goods at a lower price than craft shops and rapidly drove them out of business. Historians have traced this process in steam power and the changes in agriculture from hand tools and animal power to machine power.

The story of glass manufacturing suggests, however, that no single revolution set the course of glassmaking or glass's place in various societies. Instead, long periods of unchanging glassmaking technology alternated with short intense periods during which glass changed thinking about people's place in society and prompted actual changes in how individuals spent their time and led their lives. As a technology, modern glassmaking participated in three of these intense periods: the seventeenth-century frenzy of scientific research based on lenses, the nineteenth-century movement to incorporate large flat glass windows in retail display, and the mid-twentieth-century incorporation of large-scale flat glass in skyscrapers and in ordinary homes. It is im-portant to note that these periods of rapid change did not somehow sweep the world. All were mainly confined to the West. For example, only now—more than a century after flat glass came to retailing in Europe and the United States—have large glass shopfronts become common in cities in India.

Glassmaking is so complex and fraught with difficulty that any image of a lone in-ventor is incorrect. Instead, technological innovation was embedded in a community. Leeuwenhoek had his Royal Society of England. Plate glass came out of a designated royal glass workshop in eighteenth-century France. The only way to get the necessary expertise was to hire those with specialized knowledge. Recall that US entrepreneurs in the 1880s successfully recruited glassworkers from Belgium and France. Chemists of twentieth-century glass found a home at the Owens-Corning laboratory in Corning, New York. Technological innovations in glassmaking often required a large scale to succeed. For example, Pittsburgh Plate Glass's enormous plate glass facility succeeded where many other plants attempting to make plate glass had failed.

Developments in fields outside glass impacted technological development. Consider how the making of eighteenth-century French plate glass depended on large-scale steel rollers, which were developed for the crushing of stone. (A century later, similar rollers would constitute a new technology for printing newspapers.) Ecological and energy considerations sometimes severely hindered technological innovation. Wood-fired glassmaking kilns in England so quickly decimated forests that local governments moved to limit production. Only the use of coal overcame this barrier.

We have seen that a revolution in glassmaking technology itself never occurred. Many glass products did, however, go through their own Industrial Revolution in the nineteenth century. The manufacture of bottles for beer, whiskey, and milk became an engineered and automated process, with many patented claims for new machinery. The production of light bulbs likewise moved from a hand-blown to a fully automated process.[17]

In the twentieth century new glass formulations and technologies produced florescent lighting, X-ray plates, vacuum tubes for radios and televisions, heat-resistant glass cookware and dinnerware, safety glass for car windshields, glass block for walls, fiberglass insulation, glass piping for moving corrosive chemicals, glass for deep diving undersea vehicles, and tempered glass for shower doors, thermometers, neon signs, scientific equipment, and inexpensive mirrors. The pace of invention has only increased in this century, producing special glasses for solar panels and cell phones, fiber optics for communication, window glass coatings that prevent heat loss from homes and buildings, and glass panels that become opaque in the evening.

The discovery of a new technology in one country did not mean that it took off in the rest of the world. Older and newer technological solutions did and do coexist side by side. In India, for example, many glass objects are still made by skilled hands, not

Solar panels on a roof.

automation. There are also huge high-speed glass factories in the country that turn 350 tons of raw glass a day into bottles for the pharmaceutical sector.

The important point here is that technological innovation succeeds only if it somehow translates into local needs and usages. Indian farmers converted from plow animals to tractors only when the banking system changed to provide credit to buy a tractor. To run a tractor required a reliable supply of gasoline. Repayment of the bank loan for the tractor required rural electrification, which ran the irrigation pumps and increased yield. A technology that solves a widespread problem can also spread extraordinarily quickly. In India, cell phones—with glass screens—spread throughout society in less than a generation.

We have considered glass technology over several centuries and several locations and have found that technological innovation could not and did not drive history in any straightforward way. Just because the Romans knew how to blow glass into plates that resembled luxury rock crystal did not mean that glass dominated the market for dinnerware. To the contrary, after the collapse of the Western Roman Empire, glassmaking essentially disappeared from Europe for 700 years. In China glass found a market as a substitute for expensive jade, and there it stopped, not driving anything for a thousand years. There were times and places where glass did fit a trend or a need. Glass was certainly part of the early skyscraper construction, but the driver was limited available land in densely populated US cities, especially New York, Chicago, and Philadelphia. Glass became something of a driver only when tastes were rapidly

TIMELINE

ca. 1200 BCE
Indigenous invention of glassmaking in India

1000 BCE
Indigenous invention of glassmaking in China

965–1040 CE
Life of Alhazen, important researcher into optics

1564–1642
Life of Galileo Galilei

1608
Jacob Metius and Hans Lippershey combine a convex lens and a concave lens into a far-seeing device

1632–1723
Life of Antony van Leeuwenhoek

1674
Local Delft doctor recommends Leeuwenhoek's discoveries to the Royal Society in England

May–July 1675
Leeuwenhoek observes life in rain and well water through a microscope

changing, as in the rise of fashionable glass-fronted shops in late eighteenth-century England and the post–World War II indoor-outdoor house designs.

If technology is not a straightforward driver of history, what accounts for the search for new techniques and processes? Is the exploration of the natural world something intrinsic to humans? Is the search for a better hoe, storage pot, or weapon part of our nature? How, then, can we account for societies who have existed for centuries, even millennia, with what appears to be an unchanging technology? Or do they in fact revise and develop their core technologies in subtle ways, not noticed by literate elites? These questions and their answers are critical to our world and our future and are worth asking about new technologies as—inevitably—they arise.

For digital learning resources, please go to
www.oup.com/he/gordon-seventhemes1e

1687
New process of glassmaking that produces optically flat, smooth, and clear sheets of large glass is developed in Saint-Gobain, France

1800
Inventors work out issues with microscope lenses

ca. 1850
First efforts of US glassworks to make plate glass

1880
US entrepreneurs recruit glassmakers from Belgium and France, and US glassmaking industry successfully creates flat, bubble-free, clear glass

1920–1975
Albert Noe makes cylinder glass in southern Ohio

ca. 1930
Production of large flat glass becomes industrial and largely automated

1950
Development of float glass

Migration and the Immigrant Experience

The Big Picture: Peoples on the Move

As far back as researchers can trace early human beings and their near relatives, humans then and ever since have been on the move. *Homo erectus* in the period about 800,000 years ago moved north though the Great Rift region of eastern Africa. Some followed the Nile north and settled on the north coast of Africa and the eastern coast of the Mediterranean. Others turned east and migrated around the coast of the Arabian Peninsula, followed the coast of the Arabian Sea to India, pushed on around the Bay of Bengal to current-day mainland Southeast Asia, and eventually reached central China. At about the same time *Homo heidelbergensis* left Africa and migrated northwest into Europe and northeast into the area of the Black Sea and the Caspian Sea. The Neanderthal (possibly descendants of the *Homo heidelbergensis*) settled in northern Europe. The Denisovan migrated to the Altai Mountains of Mongolia and interbred with Neanderthal and later with our direct ancestors, *Homo sapiens*. Of all these early migrants, *Homo sapiens* traveled the farthest. They first migrated from Africa to the

Recent arrivals from Eastern Europe wait to be processed at the immigration station on Ellis Island, New York, late nineteenth century.

Arabian Peninsula more than 100,000 years ago and there interbred with Neanderthal. By 40,000 years ago they had migrated west to Europe (stopped only by the glaciers, which covered much of northern Europe), east to India, Southeast Asia, Australia, and China, and by 18,000 years ago across the land bridge to North America.

The historian Patrick Manning has argued for three features of this long period of prehistoric (that is, before written records) migration that changed humans much more than biological evolution.[1] The first is language, by which humans communicated crucial information to others of their group. Language and the sharing of information would have eased the difficult and dangerous process of migrating into a new environment: discovering edible and useful plants, identifying toxic plants, and distinguishing prey from predators. Historical linguistic evidence suggests that humans developed detailed and specific language in widely disparate locations, including Africa, the Middle East, the steppes north of Tibet, China, and Australia. The second feature of prehistoric migration was communication between groups. As migrant groups encountered previous migrants without a shared language, linguistic and DNA evidence suggests that these encounters were not necessarily violent. Genes, information, concepts, and rituals passed between groups. This practice of sharing is more efficient and less dangerous than exploring a new environment from scratch. The third feature of prehistoric migration was that it was a long, long process. Groups moved, stayed put for centuries or millennia, and then moved again. These pauses permitted a group to develop long-lasting features of a culture, such as ideas of sacred landscape, spiritual ritual, music, and burial customs. In the populating of the Americas, for example, researchers have found three relatively short periods of large-scale migration from Asia interspersed with long periods without migration.

Our focus is on migration after 1500 CE, but it is important to note some of the patterns of migration in the preceding millennium (500–1500 CE). Let us undertake a whirlwind, worldwide tour of migration, beginning in China. Migration from northern China into the southern river valleys boosted rice production. This surplus food triggered a large population increase, but transportation of the rice made possible a populous dynastic capital in the north, which could not feed itself from the surrounding countryside. The food surplus from migrants to the southern valleys fed the army, which successfully repelled repeated invasions by nomads from beyond the Great Wall and spread Chinese trade and influence west along the Silk Road.[2] Traders from South China migrated into Southeast Asia, settling in ports and marrying local women.

Moving in our tour west to India, waves of invaders first from what is now Afghanistan and later from Central Asia and Mongolia swept into South Asia and ruled North and Central India for almost a thousand years. Their courts attracted administrators, soldiers, clerics, and doctors.[3] The southern portion of the subcontinent was intimately connected to Southeast Asia, both by trade and by the export of Hindu sagas, symbolism,

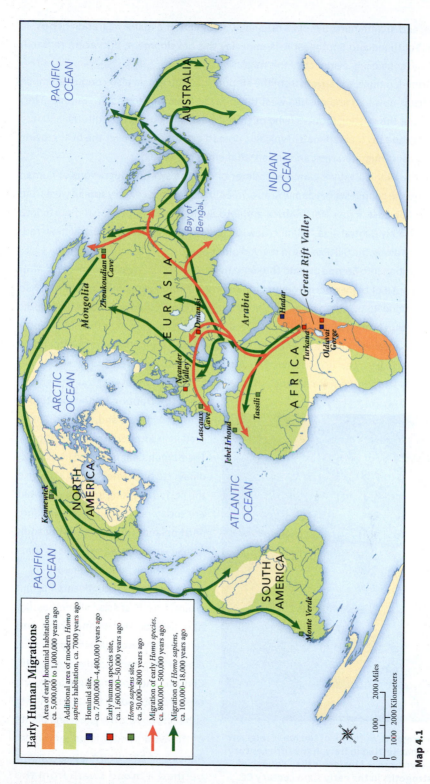

Early Human Migrations

Area of early hominid habitation, ca. 5,000,000 to 1,000,000 years ago

Additional area of modern *Homo sapiens* habitation, ca. 7000 years ago

Hominid site, ca. 7,000,000–4,400,000 years ago

Early human species site, ca. 1,600,000–50,000 years ago

Homo sapiens site, ca. 50,000–8000 years ago

Migration of early *Homo* species, ca. 800,000–500,000 years ago

Migration of *Homo sapiens*, ca. 100,000–18,000 years ago

PACIFIC OCEAN

AUSTRALIA

INDIAN OCEAN

Bay of Bengal

E U R A S I A

Mongolia

Zhoukoudian Cave

Dmanisi

Arabia

Great Rift Valley

Hadar

Turkana

Olduvai Gorge

A F R I C A

ARCTIC OCEAN

Neander Valley

Lascaux Cave

Jebel Irhoud

Tassili

NORTH AMERICA

Kennewick

ATLANTIC OCEAN

SOUTH AMERICA

Monte Verde

PACIFIC OCEAN

0   1000   2000 Miles

0   1000   2000 Kilometers

Map 4.1

gods, and architecture. Scholars originally thought that a major migration of people from South India to Southeast Asia underlay this development, but recent research finds no convincing evidence of this migration.

Armed, mounted warriors from the steppes of Central Asia also conquered much of what is now Iran and pushed west through the Caucasus to eastern Europe. They drove out the existing farmers (who migrated west) and turned agricultural land into grazing land for their animals. Typically, nomad groups fought over the best grazing land. Losers migrated west and seized what lands they could.

In the Middle East we would encounter one of the swiftest migrations of human history. The conquests by Islamic Arab armies in the seventh century spread west from the Middle East across North Africa and into Spain, east into Persia, and north into what is today Central Asia.[4] Islamic, Jewish, and Greek migrants populated new trading cities along the Silk Road and revived older ones.

Migration into Europe around the same time (500–1000) is well documented. After the collapse of the western Roman Empire around 400, many of the tribes who had lived beyond Rome's borders moved into what had been Roman provinces. Ostrogoths (the eastern branch of the Goths) migrated west from a region near the Black Sea to conquer southern Europe all the way into Italy. When their empire broke up, many migrants stayed. The Visigoths (western Goths), who had captured and sacked Rome, migrated into southern France and eventually into Spain. A variety of groups migrated from the Danube Valley westward across the Rhine and, like the Goths, settled in southern France and Spain. The Burgundians migrated from Scandinavia to the Rhine Valley. This is also the period of Viking invasions of what are today northern France, Ireland, and England. These seafaring Scandinavian warriors had specialized ships for war, trade, and settlement.

On the American continents, migrant groups from East Asia millennia earlier had crossed the Bering Strait and settled every favorable ecological niche. Along rivers and coastlines of North, Central, and South America, groups exploited abundant fish and shellfish. Other groups ate the game and plants of the woodland, plains, or jungle. Agriculture based on maize and beans defined a broad swath from the

The Ostrogoths were one of the many migrant groups that settled in Italy in the fifth century CE. Shown here is Amalasuintha, a queen of the Ostrogoths in the early sixth century CE.

Polynesian seafarers riding a twin-hulled catamaran, as shown in this nineteenth century lithograph.

Mississippi River west to California and south through Mexico and Central America. Groups in the South American highlands relied on potatoes and squash. Finding an ecological niche did not mean the end of migration—far from it. Jockeying and warfare between groups produced mass migrations, as did drought.

Moving west to the Pacific Islands, we find a longstanding pattern of migration that began with boats arriving before the Common Era in the islands closest to China. The development of twin-hulled catamarans allowed for long ocean voyages. By the period we are considering (500–1500), migrants had discovered and populated even the most remote of the Pacific Islands, such as Hawaii, Tahiti, and New Zealand.[5]

This welter of migrations raises many questions about modern migration. Has there ever been a "typical" migrant or migration? What are the motivations and impediments to migration? How does war or natural catastrophe relate to migration? How does long-distance migration differ from migration within a state or across a border? Are migrants mostly men or mostly women? How does migration change when there is no open land in which to settle? How does a migrant group or individual learn the necessary information about a new place, people, and customs? How common is intermarriage between immigrants and hosts? How does migration differ if there is little time to plan or discuss it within a family? How do refugees differ from other migrants? What portion of migrants return to their original home? Do governments create migration—subsidized, voluntary, or forced?[6]

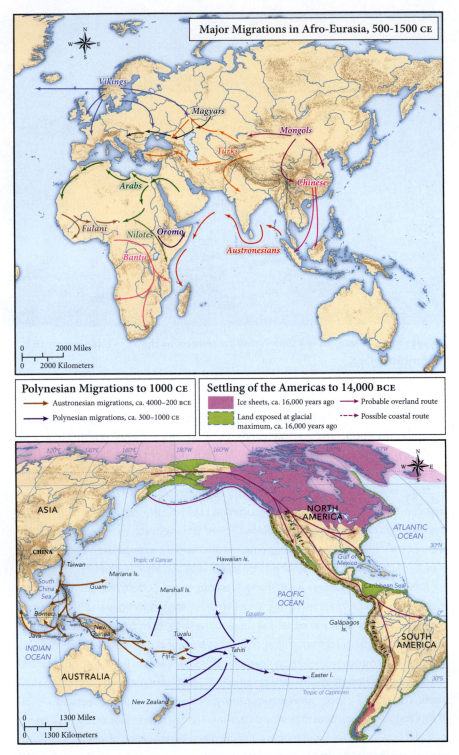

Major Migrations in Afro-Eurasia, 500–1500 CE

Polynesian Migrations to 1000 CE

→ Austronesian migrations, ca. 4000–200 BCE

→ Polynesian migrations, ca. 300–1000 CE

Settling of the Americas to 14,000 BCE

Ice sheets, ca. 16,000 years ago

Land exposed at glacial maximum, ca. 16,000 years ago

→ Probable overland route

---→ Possible coastal route

Map 4.2

Arrivals in a New Country

Our first guide to modern migration is José Ángel Navejas, a native of Guadalajara, Mexico, who entered the United States sometime in mid-1990. His thoughtful and observant memoir records seventeen years of life as an undocumented immigrant. His night trek across the border was dangerous and exhausting:

> How long we spend perched on top of that hill afterward I can't tell. . . .
> I reckon we have been going for more than an hour. All I know is I'm
> glad we stopped. A smoker at the time, I feel dizzy, my lungs are swell
> ing, my nostrils flare rapidly, my legs are getting heavier, and I am
> drenched in sweat. The coyote [human smuggler] squats and hisses at
> us not to move, gesticulating violently and pointing to the ground with
> his right hand.
>
> I land on my stomach and crawl my way into a narrow space be
> tween a big rock and a thorny bush. The backpack in which I carry a
> change of clothes, a bottle of water, and some snacks is wet with sweat,
> and I feel a pointy rock stabbing me right in the stomach, but remain
> motionless. I am panting heavily and fear that my breathing will attract
> a rattlesnake. A few minutes pass, and someone close by begins to
> snore. I keep my eyes open.[7]

José and his fellow immigrants crossed an eight-lane freeway, waded inside a sewer, passed through a back yard, and rendezvoused with a van that took them to a dilapidated house in San Diego packed with other immigrants. Before his relatives could pick José up, the border police captured him, took a deposition, and sent him back to Mexico. On his second attempt, he succeeded in disappearing into the United States. José's story is familiar, the stuff of movies and TV news reporting.

Let us compare José's experience with another immigrant to the United States. As part of her dissertation research, Emily Wang (herself an immigrant from China) interviewed several immigrant women from Middle Eastern countries. One of them, Zena (not her real name), came from Baghdad in Iraq to the United States within a year of José's misadventures in San Diego. The previous year a friend of her brother had returned from the United States to Iraq and asked for Zena in marriage. Zena's parents agreed, and at age twenty-five she married him in Baghdad. A few months later she joined her new husband in an apartment in Southfield, Michigan, a predominantly white suburb of Detroit. The interview transcript confirms that Zena's life in Iraq had been urban and, on the whole, pleasant. (Remember that she lived in Baghdad decades before the Iraq War of 2003 to 2011.)

> Well, all my life there, you know, I live in capital city [Baghdad], my life
> is similar, a lot like American people. Go with the girls, even with
> family, go on trips, shopping mall. We have small mall, not like big now,
> but when I was a teenager, small malls; we go, we shop and we have fun,
> eat ice cream. We don't have pizza there but we have hamburger and we
> have our cultural food and I live beautiful life there and I enjoy it every
> second.[8]

Zena traveled with her family to Syria, Jordan, Lebanon, and especially Turkey because "in Iraq summer is so hot and Turkey is so cool and their food is delicious and [the] country is beautiful."

Shortly after Zena arrived in Southfield, her husband's friends threw a party for the newly married couple. "And we did it in a restaurant. Everybody, almost everybody come. We enjoy; we took a lot of pictures. It was a lot of fun."

Our third guide to immigrant life is Annah Frances Acam Emuge. She was born in 1959 into the Iteso clan in the northeast semiarid portion of Uganda (in East Africa) and grew up in a village of huts surrounded by grazing land. (Her village is about a hundred miles west of the birthplace in Kenya of Jomo Kenyatta, our guide in Chapter 9.) Her family herded animals and grew staple vegetables and grains in a plot adjacent to their hut. Working in the fields, carrying water, and collecting firewood loom large in her earliest childhood memories.[9] When she was five years old her mother convinced her father that Annah must attend a primary mission school about a mile from home. A year later, at a hospital, she saw a white person for the first time, and a year after that she began walking the seven miles to the nearest secondary mission school. Her biographer writes:

> It was in fifth grade that Annah began learning that there are actually
> other continents beyond Africa. One weekend, Toto [her mother] took
> Annah to the market area of Ngora Township, where there were many
> stands set up on busy streets. Annah had never seen Ngora like this,
> since Saturday was market day. The people looked like the pictures in
> her textbooks—some were light-skinned with long blond hair, and
> there were Asians and Indians. It seemed that all of them were either
> selling or buying something, and many of them were loudly disputing
> the price of a sparkling trinket or a ripe, juicy mango.[10]

There were years of drought and sickness within the family. Still, she treasured school and persevered, despite taking on many of the tasks of her ailing mother.

Annah passed the secondary-school exams and moved from her village to a Baptist college town two hours away by bus. Her oldest sister, a nurse, lived in the town with her husband, who worked in government service. They owned a concrete blockhouse with a metal roof, which seemed like a palace to Annah, who would live with them during her first two college years.[11] She then transferred to a premier college 125 miles from her village. These college years overlapped the brutal dictatorship of Uganda's Idi Amin (r. 1974–1983). He sent his army to attack Christians, schools, and even those who spoke English. He pitted Uganda's northern tribes against the southern tribes.

General Idi Amin speaks at a military parade, January 1975.

Conditions deteriorated, and trucks full of bodies rumbled by the college. One truck stopped, and the soldiers took all the food, leaving none for the students or staff. By this point,

> Rosemary [Annah's older sister] had learned of an internship offered by the hospital in Olio (in eastern Uganda) where she had once worked as a nurse, and Annah had carefully written a letter of application, which her elder sister had corrected and then submitted. This step felt right to Annah, but still she worried about leaving school for a semester, even for more learning. Was this truly the path she should be taking?[12]

During Annah's two-year internship at the hospital, the situation became desperate. Bands of soldiers roamed through the countryside, raping, stealing, and killing. Every night the staff of the hospital and a nearby school scattered into the village's surrounding scrub to avoid capture. Finally, in 1983, Idi Amin was overthrown, but the country did not return to "normal." There was no normal. People were starving. The soldiers had burned the busses. With no medicines or hospital equipment, the doctors and nurses could do nothing for patients.[13] United Nation relief efforts were late and often deficient.

At eighteen, Annah married the head of the mission school, who was nine years older. She had her first child that year. Regional animosities were even stronger than under Idi Amin. A nearby group often sent armed cattle raiders through the Iteso districts. For months Annah and her husband James once again hid in the scrub trees and bushes at night. James took a government job as inspector of regional schools and traveled in a government car, which was relatively safe. He left Annah and the children alone for days at a time. In 1983, the education department offered to send James overseas for graduate work in educational administration (with the suggestion that he would be education minister when he returned). Annah and the children would accompany him. So, in 1983, the family left the violence of Uganda for the leafy campus of Ohio University in Athens, Ohio.

As our three guides reveal, there is no typical immigrant. Life stories vary greatly, even among immigrants arriving at the same time from the same country. Immigrants vary by class, gender, and education; their familiarity with the language of the new country; their rural, urban, or suburban backgrounds; and their religious or secular upbringing.

Al Houda Supermarket, Dearborn, Michigan.

José, Zena, and Annah all knew where they were going and why. José sought an enclave, and Zena found herself in an enclave—that is, a community or neighborhood with many people like themselves.[14] These enclaves figure prominently in all immigration of the nineteenth and twentieth centuries. Larger cities had neighborhoods known as Little Italy or Chinatown. In the United States, Milwaukee was famous for its German immigrants and the beer they brewed. German newspapers and social clubs flourished. Many Scandinavians came to Minneapolis and Duluth, Minnesota, where Swedish newspapers and schools thrived. This pattern has continued. A few Hmong immigrants came from Vietnam to Minneapolis on the 1980s, and thousands followed the original settlers. Somali immigrants have established ethnic enclaves in Minneapolis and Columbus, Ohio. Cubans settled in Miami's "Little Havana" and produced Spanish-language newspapers and television stations.

If the "where to" of immigrants is important, so is the "when." Immigration policy changed quickly, opening or closing opportunities for various ethnic groups. If José had decided a century earlier, in 1890, that opportunities were better in California than in Mexico, he would have simply walked across the border and contacted relatives on the US side. After all, California had been part of Mexico about a half-century earlier, and people still casually crossed the border in both directions. By the last decades of the nineteenth century California's agriculture needed large numbers of seasonal Hispanic labor—men and women—to plant, weed, and harvest crops. Woody Guthrie, the brilliant balladeer from Oklahoma, sang about this work in the 1930s:

> I worked in your orchards of peaches and prunes
> Slept on the ground in the light of your moon
> On the edge of the city you'll see us and then
> We come with the dust and we go with the wind
>
> California and Arizona, I make all your crops
> And it's North up to Oregon to gather your hops
> Dig the beets from your ground, cut the grapes from your vine
> To set on your table your light sparkling wine[15]

It is important to emphasize that in the expanding economy of late nineteenth-century California, families of Hispanic background owned general goods and hardware stores, ranches, farms, orchards, and factories. They also worked in furniture factories and construction. Migrant Hispanic workers may have been poor, but many Hispanics settled in California were not. They were instead part of a complex, layered society with upper, middle, and lower classes.

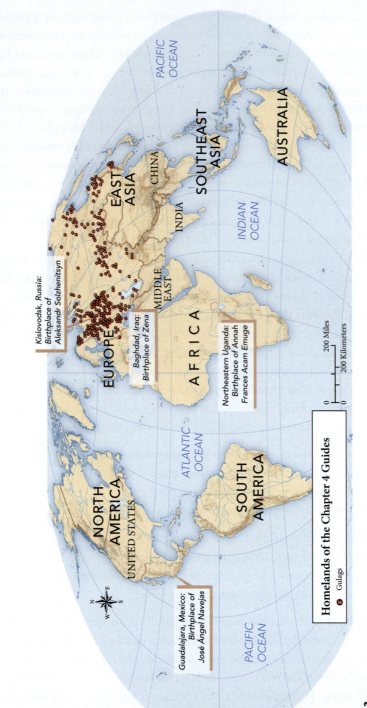

PACIFIC OCEAN

AUSTRALIA

CHINA

EAST ASIA

SOUTHEAST ASIA

INDIA

INDIAN OCEAN

MIDDLE EAST

AFRICA

Kislovodsk, Russia:
Birthplace of
Aleksandr Solzhenitsyn

EUROPE

Baghdad, Iraq:
Birthplace of Zena

Northeastern Uganda:
Birthplace of Annah
Frances Acam Emuge

200 Miles

200 Kilometers

0

0

ATLANTIC OCEAN

SOUTH AMERICA

NORTH AMERICA

UNITED STATES

Homelands of the Chapter 4 Guides

● Gulags

Guadalajara, Mexico:
Birthplace of
José Ángel Navejas

PACIFIC OCEAN

N
E
S
W

Map 4.3

Global Mass Migration and Its Constraints

If someone like Zena had migrated to America a century earlier (around 1900), she would have been part of the largest mass migration in human history, which included British, Irish, Germans, Italians, Poles, Greeks, eastern Europeans, Russians, and Scandinavians. Several features of this migration are important.[16] First, some European governments saw migration as a solution to (or at least the export of) social problems—rural and urban poverty, the overcrowding of cities, drunkenness, prostitution, and troublesome minorities. England publicized opportunities in Canada, the United States, Australia, and South Africa and often paid for passage of immigrants. Other European governments, however, especially Germany, discouraged or even banned migration, fearing it would drain the country of military recruits. Second, steam ships replaced sailing ships, drastically cutting the time of transoceanic voyages and increasing the safety of passages. Shipping lines quickly figured out that immigrants were the most profitable segment of their business. First-class passengers might appreciate the glamour of a ship—its wood paneling, mirrored walls, library, smoking room, and gourmet meals—but it was down in steerage, jammed with low-fare migrants and their belongings, that the shipping line made money. Here is a description of the typical accommodations in steerage:

> Follow me now into the compartment in which I have discovered
> "Berth No. 25." It is a space two yards long by one broad, and to the left
> and right of this rise three more tiers of bunks. There are twenty of
> them in the compartment and into each one the future occupant is
> busy putting what bedding he has provided himself as the company
> provides nothing except space and victuals [food].[17]

To fill the steerage berths, shipping lines sent recruiters into the countryside carrying colorful brochures highlighting the opportunities of a new country. The recruiters attracted landless laborers, but also families owning a small plot of land; they were only one bad harvest away from starvation. Third, the spread of rail lines inland from ports allowed families—if they could afford the fare—to reach the port more easily and quickly. Fourth, "chain migration" was the norm. One brave migrant went to Adelaide or Capetown or Toronto and wrote back to his or her family on conditions in the new country. If the situation was promising, other family members followed.[18]

In the mass migration of the late nineteenth century, the number of immigrants from the Muslim Middle East was small. The first were single men from Lebanon and Syria, who worked in factories in New England and the Midwest. Their numbers in any location were too small to establish a mosque. Had

Migrants from Europe jam the deck of a boat as it approaches Ellis Island in New York Harbor, ca. 1900.

someone like Zena married one of these workers, life would have been hard. Wages were low, and small-town racial prejudice ran deep. At the same time, Annah's story would not have been possible in the late nineteenth century, when Africans were explicitly excluded from entering the United States by racial restriction laws.

A couple of decades into the twentieth century, the possibilities of emigration to the United States dramatically declined. In response to fears of Catholic eastern European immigrants and possible Communists among the Russian immigrants, Congress passed laws severely restricting immigration. Still deemed acceptable were "whites" from the Western Hemisphere but not "Asians," which included Chinese, Japanese, Indians, and all Africans.

For decades, male researchers dominated the field of migration studies. They assumed that men were the key actors in migration—that women and children "accompanied" them. As women joined the field of migration studies and focused their research on women, this assumption turned out to be wrong. First, women were present in all migrations, whether from England to Australia, Europe to Brazil, Ireland to Canada, or China to Malaya. Second, women often

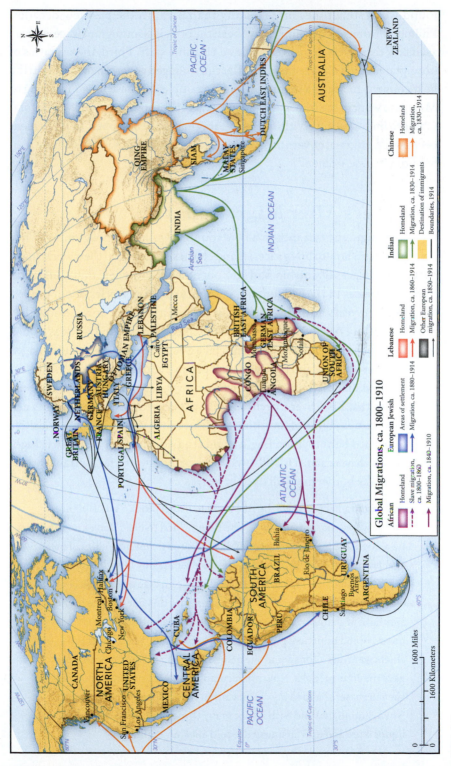

Global Migrations, ca. 1800–1910

African

Homeland

Slave migration, ca. 1800–1860

Migration, ca. 1860–1910

European Jewish

Homeland

Areas of settlement

Migration, ca. 1880–1914

Lebanese

Homeland

Migration, ca. 1880–1914

Other European migration, ca. 1850–1914

Indian

Homeland

Migration, ca. 1860–1914

Destination of immigrants

Boundaries, 1914

Chinese

Homeland

Migration, ca. 1830–1914

Map 4.4

found work, sometimes more readily than men. In the past few decades, Philippine women, for example, have been the principal immigrant wage-earners as maids, caregivers in institutions, and cleaning staff. Third, the sex ratios of immigrants could change rapidly, reflecting changed government policy in the host country. In Malaya in mid-1930, for example, Chinese men migrating to Malaya to work in the mines and plantations constituted 75 percent of the total Chinese immigration. Within a few years that figure dropped to 43 percent because the colonial government of Malaya legislated quotas on Chinese men but not Chinese women.[19]

The Years After Migration

For all immigrants, entrance to a new country was just the beginning. They needed to learn how to buy groceries and clothes, understand their work, make friends, find places of worship, and seek out other places where they could relax from the stresses of the encounter. Let us return to the stories of our guides, say five to ten years after their arrival in the United States, and see how they were doing. José Ángel Navejas moved to Chicago and found work as a cook in a Mexican restaurant. After buying a fake Social Security card, he managed to get a driver's license and purchase an inexpensive used car. Then, new identification laws made it impossible for José to travel, especially by air, as he could not be sure that his driver's license would pass muster. Navejas sold his car. There was no possibility of returning to Mexico for a visit. Still, on the positive side, he pushed hard to learn English and studied and passed his GED high-school equivalency exam. He still owed much of the coyote's fee for transporting him across the border and still lived in fear:

> Busy amid a hectic crowd, he [the store manager] took a quick glance and gestured disapprovingly. . . . He then turned to me. I don't know if he recognized me, but my week-old beard surely convinced him of my age. He drew a complicit smirk—yes, he'd let me buy my wine, but I wasn't fooling him. He knew full well I carried a fake document. . . . He wouldn't call the police on me. He'd simply let this one minute in the spotlight of shame be my lesson. I stood there, a line of five or six inquisitive and impatient people waiting behind me. The adjacent cashiers were just as busy, and the people standing in line on both sides gave me strange looks. Now my accomplice, the manager, authorized the purchase. I handed my credit card to the cashier and my receipt. Then, humiliated and with a knot in my throat, I stepped out of the liquor store and into an unusually cold autumn night.[20]

José writes of his growing awareness of how psychologically to survive:

> I've grown used to living in the shadows. Although it is plagued with
> inconveniences, I've learned to embrace this lifestyle wholeheartedly. If
> I had to, I'd choose to live it all over again—every single moment of it!
> I've come to appreciate the anonymity. I love the permissiveness to slip
> in and out of places virtually unnoticed.... There is ample room for
> growth in the shadows. Although it took me a long time, I have finally
> realized that one can actually thrive in the shadows as well as anywhere
> else. Except that down here you evolve differently--you become darker,
> you grow antennae, your senses get sharper, and, best of all, you learn
> not to take things so seriously.[21]

José graduated college in Chicago, became a talented translator, and rented an
apartment in a downtown high rise. His fear of exposure as an undocumented
Mexican rose with his economic progress. He turned down jobs that required
travel, fearing discovery of his fake driver's license. He never went for drinks
with work colleagues. It would take only one hostile bartender to trigger the
collapse of his entire world, ending with deportation.

He had never been able to visit his family and friends in Guadalajara. On
Skype he finally saw his mother:

> Seventeen years had passed since we'd last seen each other face-to-face.
> In more than one sense, though, my mother was still the same woman
> who had seen me off at the bus terminal in Guadalajara. Her sad, brown
> eyes, accustomed to early departures, her mouth, always hesitant to
> smile too much and too jovially. My brother opened the blinds, and I
> saw her more clearly: some gray hairs tangled around her curls, and the
> first signs of aging adorned her brow. She bit her lower lip. I asked her
> what she'd just been doing, and she answered laundry, as usual. She
> lifted up the lower end of her apron and wiped her cheek.[22]

And what of Zena, married to a legal Iraqi immigrant? There were tensions
between the world she left and the one in which she now lived. In Baghdad she
wore jeans and T-shirts, never the hijab. In Southfield, Michigan, her husband
wanted Zena to wear the hijab. She thought about how she felt and decided
that she respected the religious traditions surrounding the hijab. She would
wear it:

> T-shirt and jeans I don't wear outside; I wear inside [the house].
> Nothing change. I am same person, you know, when I grow up.... I
> hope to stay like that.

Zena misses the bathing beach in Baghdad that was only for women. She and her friends could wear any swimwear, even a bikini, and splash and play in the water.

From her experience with American schools, Zena felt that students disregarded their teachers. She tried hard to imbue her children with respect for their teachers: "I say when I was at school, when we saw teacher come, we arise for him. . . . it is important because this is how I grow up."

Her two boys and younger daughter do not speak Arabic but understand it. Her older daughter attended Islamic schools for a couple of years and speaks Arabic. Zena frequently talked with her children about proper values and correct decorum:

> We don't do sleep over, they are welcome to come to our house but I
> don't like my girls and my boys to sleep over . . . I don't know their cul-
> tures. I don't feel safe. . . . I maybe a picky mom.

Zena has always had the dream of going to college, but she found the GED exam too difficult. She has decided to return to studying for it when her children are in college. Zena has applied for US visas for her mother, sister, and brother but is resolved to a ten-year wait.

Let us now turn to the third of our guides during her first ten years in the United States. We left Annah Emuge, her husband James, and their two small children in Athens, Ohio. James seemed to have a secure academic future. The couple had friends among the Ohio University faculty, who regularly included them in social events. Their children played with those of other faculty members. A high-level position in the Ministry of Education awaited James's return to Uganda.

This expectation collapsed with a single letter. The Education Ministry informed James that it would no longer support his graduate work in the United States. Ohio University offered to provide a tuition fellowship, but could not support the family's living expenses.[23] The family had no savings and knew no one in Uganda who could help them. James's student visa would be revoked if he could not show that he could support his family while attending college. A sympathetic official at the Ugandan Embassy sent a small amount of cash, and the family moved to smaller, cheaper housing. James's classwork was almost completed, and he decided to go to work to maintain the family while he finished his dissertation. The only job he could find was making sandwiches in a fast food restaurant in Columbus, seventy-five miles away. Money was running out.

A coup in Uganda made it impossible for the family to return home. The new dictator hated their Iteso ethnic group. The military burned villages, and killings once again became frequent. James found a job at a convenience store in Washington, DC and moved the family there. He began to drink heavily, however, and was arrested for drunken driving. The family moved into a seedy motel. Annah found work at a local McDonald's, but her husband disappeared for days at a time, forcing Annah and her children to find temporary shelter in an emergency refugee center. A sympathetic lawyer helped her file refugee papers, which gave both parents six-month work certificates and qualified the family for food stamps. Soon after James returned from Washington, he loaded his wife and (now four) children into the car and moved to St. Louis, where he hoped to finish his dissertation.[24]

James Emuge steadily deteriorated and eventually died of alcoholism. Annah worked to support her family. She earned a green card and eventually became a US citizen. All of her children have graduated from college. Today she lives in St. Louis and heads a nonprofit organization that houses, feeds, and educates hundreds of children orphaned by Uganda's civil wars and AIDS epidemic.

As we have seen, each of our three guides had his or her own immigrant experience. In their first decade of life in the United States, both José and Annah were under serious stress. Either could have been deported at any time, and the jobs they could take paid little. Both had consistently to monitor bills in Congress, which might make their situation easier or more difficult, and both understood that education was essential to improving their situation. Recall that Annah managed to obtain refugee status so that she was able to work legally. Both passed their GED exams and went to college. By contrast, Zena could have worked legally after arriving in the United States, but she had two small children to raise and a husband who could support her. She did not pass her GED and did not fulfill her dream of going to college. Her stress was more cultural than economic. She wanted to train her children in ethics and behavior that she valued. She faced hard choices, especially when the family lived in the Detroit suburb of Southfield, surrounded by whites. Her life was easier when the family moved to the nearby city of Dearborn, a Middle Eastern enclave with signs in Arabic and all the foods and spices she desired. Let us now turn from these stories of difficult struggles and wearing times to a quite different migration, the mass forced migrations of the twentieth century.

Involuntary Mass Migration

For a complete picture of migration, we must consider the history of mass forced migrations. Several are familiar. The transatlantic slave trade delivered millions of workers to North, Central, and South America. The US

Prisoners arrive at Auschwitz-Birkenau Nazi death camp, 1944.

government decimated the First Nation peoples and forced those who survived onto reservations. Britain forced African tribes onto reservations in what is today Tanzania, Kenya, and Uganda. Britain also compelled debtors and criminals to immigrate to Australia.[25] Nazi dictator Adolf Hitler rounded up millions of Jews, Gypsies, Slavs, intellectuals, artists, and academics for transport to death camps.

In the twentieth century, for the first time governments enforced mass migration of *their own citizens*. Hitler was not the only dictator to use mass migration to isolate and kill his perceived internal enemies. Communist rulers Mao Zedong in the People's Republic of China and Joseph Stalin in the Soviet Union arrested massive numbers of their citizens and sent them to "re-education" camps, where millions died. Let us briefly consider Stalin's enormous chain of prisons, which destroyed the lives of millions of Soviet citizens. Our guide is Aleksandr Solzhenitsyn, a novelist and playwright who was interned in Stalin's camps for eight years. The descent into prison began with arrest:

> The sharp nighttime ring or rude knock at the door. The insolent entrance of unwiped jackboots of the unsleeping State Security

operatives. . . . The traditional image of arrest is also trembling hands packing for the victim—a change of underwear, a piece of soap, something to eat; and no one knows what is needed, what is permitted, what clothes are best to wear, and the Security agents keep interrupting and hurrying you. The traditional image of arrest is also what happens after, when the poor victim has been taken away. It is an alien, and crushing force totally dominating the apartment for hours on end, a breaking, ripping open, pulling from the walls, emptying things from wardrobes and desks onto the floor, shaking, dumping out, and ripping apart—piling up mountains of litter on the floor—and the crunch of things being trampled beneath jackboots.[26]

Aleksandr Solzhenitsyn, 1974.

Interrogation and torture awaited everyone arrested. Their families did not know where the prisoner was located or even if they were alive or dead. The prisoner entered a different kind of country, what Solzhenitsyn terms the "Gulag Archipelago," the connected chain of mass prisons across the Soviet Union. Stalin developed large civilian bureaucracies to run the gulags and special military forces to control them. The mass arrests swept up teachers, intellectuals, researchers, labor leaders, students, engineers, those who spoke English, and perfectly ordinary people implicated by their neighbors:

> The overall detained population in the camps, colonies, prisons, and internal exile reached a maximum in the early 1950s well in excess of 5 million people. Throughout the Stalin era, some 18 million people passed through the prisons and camps of the Gulag . . . 800,000 people were [put] to death by the Soviet secret police. . . . Furthermore, no fewer than 1.6 million died in the appalling conditions of the Gulag camps. We will never know for certain how many died during the process of exile, but that number also likely exceeds 1 million people.[27]

What was the justification for these prisons and the arrests that filled them? Scholars have debated economic motives, with many arguing that Stalin expanded the camp system to boost industrialization in the Soviet Union and access to valuable natural resources such as timber, coal, and other minerals. Yet the prisons were never an efficient use of labor, even when compared to the Soviet Union's relatively inefficient industries. The prisoners mainly built prison camps and the railroads that served them. Researchers have also dismissed the idea that Stalin's prisons were solely death camps, on the model of Hitler's concentration camps. Stalin did not primarily round up ethnic or religious groups with the intention of exterminating them. Internal documents suggest that the motivation for the prisons was Stalin's determination to purge the Soviet regime of all "enemies of the state" and to transform the Soviet Union into a global power. He was also afraid that if its society was not radically reformed, European powers would invade and conquer the Soviet Union. Anyone perceived as holding back the reforms was thrown into the gulag. Living conditions were appalling, and food was scarce. Nevertheless, about 20 percent of

Concert band of the Solovki prison camp. Part of the Gulag Archipelago, Solovki was located on the remote and desolate White Sea in northern Russia.

the gulag prisoners were released each year. The prison bureaucracy determined that these men and women had been successfully "retrained" and would no longer hinder the radical transformation of society.[28] Fortunately, these experiments in mass enforced migration to imprisonment have not been duplicated in over half a century, at least on the scale of Mao, Hitler, and Stalin. So how does migration shape our world today?

The Bigger Picture

Migration in the Twenty-First Century

Despite much rhetoric on the "flood" of migrants across the world today, the reality is that on average less than 3 percent of the world's population lives in a country different from their birth country. Of these, many will earn some money and return to their home country; others will move on to yet another country. Who are these migrants? They are job seekers, brides, family members, professionals, refugees, retirees, wealthy people who buy permanent residence, and students who overstay their visas. The countries that draw the most migrants are the United States, Canada, Australia, and Germany, though tens of thousands of temporary workers are resident in the Persian Gulf emirates and countries. Most migrant jobs fall under the category of the "3Ds"—dirty, difficult, and dangerous. Simple economic theory suggests that people move when there is a low cost to reach a location that yields higher wages. Unfortunately, this single model cannot explain a myriad of real-world situations. Wages in Greece, for example, are half of what they are in Luxemburg, but the population of Greece does not flock to Luxemburg. Much data suggest that migration is often not an individual choice but rather a strategic family decision. Families tap into informal flows of information on job possibilities and situations from "pioneer" migrants. Migrants often follow well-established routes, such as from a former colony to the colonizing country (Algeria to France or the Philippines to the United Sates). Nearly all migrants have a job lined up before they enter a new country, legally or illegally. On arrival they stay with a family member, friend, coreligionist, or member of their ethnic group.

Their stories raise a host of questions about migration and immigration. What exactly is the difference between migration and immigration? This chapter has used the terms as defined in nearly all dictionaries: "migration" refers to the act of *moving* to a new place and "immigration" to the act of *entering* a new place to live (in contrast to "emigration," which refers to the act of *leaving* a homeland). Yet the meanings of "migration" and "immigration" have become politicized—for example, to differentiate US citizens moving from Chicago to Albuquerque (migration) from foreigners moving across a national border from Mexico to the United States (immigration). Overall, in the United States and other Western nations the term "immigration" has taken on overtones of poverty, refugee status, and desperation.

More useful than the terms "migrant" and "immigrant" are four categories of legal status in US courts: (1) *Citizens* by birth or naturalization are entitled to full rights, for example, the right to vote and equal employment opportunity. (2) *Green card holders* are entitled to work and live permanently in the United States. Most people in this category are either sponsored by their family or an employer or convince a court of the dangers that would face them on return to their home country, triggering the judgment of refugee status. (3) *Temporary residents* include students, business visitors, tourists, and people engaged to marry US citizens. All temporary residents must have visas. (4) *Undocumented people* include temporary residents who overstay their visas and those who enter the United States at places other than official border crossings. They are not legally entitled to work or to social benefits such as subsidized healthcare or a driver's license. Where in this list would you place each of the guides to immigrant life in this chapter? What does each term imply about the person or group making the move?

Immigration is a worldwide phenomenon that raises a host of questions. What sort of legislation can make an immigrant into an "illegal"? Why are some people who cross borders suddenly criminals? Does immigration generally boost the economy of the host country and create more jobs than it takes away? Much current-day immigration is from Africa to Europe. How do immigration policies differ among the countries of the European Union? What does a "brain drain" mean, and does it still exist? If capital can move to the most profitable situation anywhere in the world, why can't labor? In what ways do immigrants change a host country? Is immigration inevitable for host countries with low birth rates and aging populations? What does assimilation mean, and who gets to decide?

The United Nations has recently made a promising start toward a worldwide perspective on these issues. After years of negotiation the member states have agreed to common definitions of crucial terms and policies, which are embodied in a document titled *Global Compact for Safe, Orderly and Regular Migration.* This hopeful document lays out goals for member states and actions to implement these goals in a realistic and transparent way. Consider a few paragraphs from the *Compact* on goals:[29]

> Migration has been part of the human experience throughout history, and we recognize that it is a source of prosperity, innovation and sustainable development in our globalized world. . . . No country can address the challenges and opportunities of this global phenomenon on its own. . . . We acknowledge our shared responsibilities to one another as Member States of the United Nations to address each other's needs and concerns over migration, and an overarching obligation to respect, protect and fulfill the human rights of all migrants, regardless of migration status, while promoting the security and prosperity of all our communities.[30]
>
> . . . .
>
> This Global Compact is the product of unprecedented review of evidence and data gathered during an open, transparent and inclusive process. We shared our realities and heard diverse voices, enriching and shaping our common understanding of this complex phenomenon. We learned that migration is a defining feature of our globalized world, connecting societies within and across all regions, making us all countries of origin, transit and destination.
>
> This Global Compact recognizes that safe, orderly and regular migration works for all when it takes place in a well informed, planned and consensual manner. Migration should never be an act of desperation. When it is, we must cooperate to respond to the needs to create conditions that allow communities and individuals to live in safety and dignity in their own countries. We must save lives and keep migrants out of harm's way. We must empower migrants to become full members of our societies, highlight their positive certainty for States, communities and migrants alike. To achieve this, we commit to facilitate and ensure safe, orderly and regular migration for the benefit of all.[31]

We are all migrants, whether we arrived ten years ago or 3,000 years ago. Humans have always moved: to seek new opportunities, to escape war, to practice their religious beliefs. Attempts to "seal borders" or otherwise prevent migration ultimately fail. It is useful to recall that the enormous human effort over many centuries to build the Great

Wall of China did not keep out the nomads from the north. Neither, in Roman times, did Hadrian's Wall across the whole of England keep out the Scots to the north. More productive is to think of migrants as sources of creativity, entrepreneurship, and strength for any country.

Implementing the United Nations' *Global Compact for Safe, Orderly and Regular Migration* would affect not just immigrants, but everyone in every country in the world.

TIMELINE

ca. 1890
People are able to cross the border between Mexico and California on a casual basis

ca. 1900
Mass migration of British, Irish, Germans, Italians, Poles, Greeks, Russians, and Scandinavians to America

1918–2008
Life of Aleksandr Solzhenitsyn

1924
The Immigration Act of 1924 severely restricts immigration

ca. 1930–1950s
Population transfers in the Soviet Union under Joseph Stalin

ca. 1950
Over 3 million people are in camps, colonies, prisons, and internal exile in the Soviet Union

1974–1983
Dictatorship of Uganda's Idi Amin

It is a roadmap of possible answers to many of the questions raised in this chapter, and its terms are surely worth discussion. For don't we all want to live in a world that acknowledges the "human rights of all migrants, regardless of migration status, while promoting the security and prosperity of all our communities"?

For digital learning resources, please go to
www.oup.com/he/gordon-seventhemes1e

1983
Annah Frances Acam Emuge and family leave Uganda for Ohio University in Athens, Ohio

ca. 1995
José Ángel Navejas enters the United States as an undocumented immigrant

ca. 1996
Zena, an immigrant from Baghdad, joins her husband in a mostly white suburb of Detroit, Michigan

Slavery

Old and New

The Big Picture: Slavery's Long History

In the long sweep of world history, slavery—the demeaning taint of owning, mistreating, and brutalizing people without recourse—has been one of the most central features of human societies. Absolute power over another human corrupts the owner as much as it degrades the slave. Implied and actual violence associated with slavery permeate notions of masculinity. Sexual exploitation of slaves affects concepts of gender long after slavery has been legally abolished. Legal systems attempted to define every possible encounter between slave and free citizen, to separate slaves and free citizens morally, emotionally, and physically. These efforts inevitably failed as slavery's permutations of power, lust, class, and inheritance played out over generations. Indeed, slavery was a "normal," legal, and accepted feature of every society on earth from at least the dawn of cities in the fourth century BCE until the universal abolition of slavery in the nineteenth century CE. One can explore the his-

> Enslaved persons in Rome often wore iron collars around their necks so they could be identified if they escaped. This example from the fourth century CE reads, "I have run away. Catch me. If you return me to my master Zominus you will receive a gold coin as a reward."

An enslaved Korean man strains to lift a giant bale of straw tied to his back, ca. 1903.

tory of Southeast Asia, the Americas, Russia, Europe, the Middle East, or the Pacific Islands and find one or another version of slavery. One measure of just how morally accepted slavery was across the premodern world is the astonishing fact that none of the founders of the world's most widespread religions and influential philosophies condemned it: not the Buddha, not the writers of the Hindu sacred texts, not the authors of the Torah or of the Talmud, not Christ, not Muhammad, and not Confucius, Socrates, Plato, or Aristotle. Across the world slaves have performed much of the ordinary labor in agriculture and herding and the hard, dirty, and dangerous labor in mines. They rowed ships, constructed buildings, and built roads. Much of the arduous work in households—cleaning, food preparation, laundry, and carrying water—was performed by slaves. Slaves have also been the soldiers in many armies, teachers in the households of elites, concubines, overseers of other slaves, and even civil officials endowed with a high degree of authority.

Most enslaved persons were captured in war. The Book of Deuteronomy (in the Hebrew Bible), which dates from around the seventh century BCE, makes clear that female war captives from distant cities could expect permanent enslavement, as could their children:

> When the LORD your God delivers it [a city] into your hand, put to the sword all the men in it. As for the women, the children, the livestock and everything else in the city, you may take these as plunder for yourselves. And you may use the plunder the LORD your God gives you from your enemies. This is how you are to treat all the cities that are at a distance from you and do not belong to the nations nearby.[1]

It was the same elsewhere—for example, in early China. War captives could expect a life of physical labor and no rights:

> The great state marshals its armies of boats and chariots to attack a blameless country. . . . The people who resist are beheaded, those who do not resist are put in bonds and brought back. The men are made drivers and grooms. The women are made grinders of corn [wheat].[2]

Slavery has been described in a multitude of languages, legal codes, philo-sophical essays, poems, and stories and defies a simple definition. Nevertheless, across human history there have been some common features of slavery. A slave was generally cut off from friends and family and taken to a place where he or she occupied the bottom rung of the social ladder. The "master" generally held the slave as property (like sheep or cattle) with broad control over his or her living conditions, labor, and social contacts. In many forms of slavery the master controlled marriage. In practice he bred the slaves for bigger and stronger offspring (parallel to breeding animals). Violence—lashings and shackles—followed any breach of the rules. In essence, the master owned the enslaved person's body.[3]

Our guide to a life in slavery and freedom is Esteban Montejo. He was born into Cuban slavery in 1860, twenty-six years before Spain abolished slavery in its colony. In 1965, at age 105, he told stories of his life and times to a Cuban anthropologist named Miguel Barnet. Esteban's memoir is important because there are so few memoirs of slavery in the Caribbean. It is even more important because he lived through the tran-sition from slavery to freedom, and his memoir is remarkably clear on the complexity of slavery and the limited effects of its legal end.[4]

Witnesses, Memoirs, and Primary Sources

Yet Esteban's eyewitness account is not some perfect recounting of the past. Miguel Barnet, the anthropologist who interviewed him, acknowledges in the introduction to the memoir that Esteban was initially reluctant to talk about his life. The anthropologist had to gain Esteban's trust before he would speak at all. Barnet "filled shoeboxes with notes and filing cards" and "taped a lot" (but not all) of their conversations.[5] Barnet asked questions that interested him as an anthropologist, such as the social life of slaves and especially Esteban's life as a runaway. At the end of two years of conversations Barnet reviewed all his notes and tapes, cut a lot for concision, and reorganized the material into a single story:

> I wanted his story to sound spontaneous and as if it came from the heart, and so I inserted words and expressions characteristic of Esteban wherever they seemed appropriate . . . I have necessarily had to para-phrase a good deal of what he told me. If I had transcribed his story word for word it would have been confusing and repetitive.[6]

Barnet's recasting of Esteban's stories does not cast doubt on the overall authenticity of the narrative, but it does force us to consider carefully the term "primary source," or firsthand account. People have always had a reason to write

Esteban Montejo, *The Autobiography of a Runaway Slave*.

about what they have experienced, whether for a specific purpose like bearing witness to an important event or just because they enjoy telling stories of their lives.

Barnet, who rearranged and edited his notes and recordings, was well aware of what he was doing and did as much as possible to strengthen the authenticity of the narrative. He permitted Esteban to read his notes, and he checked the facts of Esteban's account by talking with other old men and combing the local and state archives.

Plantation Slavery, from the Perspectives of Esteban and History

Esteban's rich human story begins with his early years:

> Like all children born into slavery . . . I was born in an infirmary [a large wooden hut] where they took the pregnant Negresses to give birth. I think that it was the Santa Teresa plantation, but I am not sure. I do remember my godparents talking a lot about this plantation and its owners, people called La Ronda. . . . Negroes were sold like pigs, and they sold me at once, which is why I remember nothing of the place.[7]

> . . . .

> A child of good stock cost five hundred pesos, that is of strong, tall parents. Tall Negroes were privileged. The masters picked them out to mate with tall, healthy women and shut them up together in the barracoons [slave quarters] and forced them to sleep together. The women had to produce healthy babies every year. I tell you, it was like breeding animals.[8]

Enslaved men and women cutting sugarcane, Antigua, 1823.

At ten years old Esteban began work as a driver of a *bagasse* wagon, moving loads of sugarcane from which the juice had been extracted. *Bagasse* was the fuel of the plantation, burned to heat the steam engines, which ran the rollers to crush the cane and extract the juice. Slaves also shoveled bagasse to fuel three furnaces, which evaporated the juice into refined sugar.

Most slaves lived in filthy and crowded barracks, or barraccoons:

> Around two hundred slaves of all colours lived in the Flor de Sagua barracoon. This was laid out in rows facing each other with a door in the middle and a massive padlock to shut the slaves in at night. There were barracoons of wood and barracoons of masonry with tiled roofs. Both types had mud floors and were dirty as hell. And there was no modern ventilation there! Just a hole in the wall or a small barred window. The result was that the place swarmed with fleas and ticks, which made the inmates ill.[9]

> ....

> You caught lots of illnesses in the barraccoons, in fact men got sicker than anywhere else. It was not unusual to find a Negro with as many as three sicknesses at once. If it wasn't colic it was whooping cough. Colic

gave you a pain in the gut which lasted a few hours and left you shagged. Whooping cough and measles were catching. But the worst sicknesses, which made a skeleton of everyone, was smallpox and the black sickness [cholera]. Smallpox left men all swollen, and the black sickness took them by surprise; it struck suddenly and between one bout of vomiting and the next you ended up a corpse.[10]

To understand fully this form of plantation slavery it is important to place the day-to-day suffering of slaves like Esteban in larger context. The sociologist André Gunder Frank has studied Caribbean plantations from a world-systems perspective.[11] He points out that the workers were slaves, forcibly brought in, and the machines to extract juice were produced overseas. The entire economic model was an integral extension of European colonialism and capitalism. The venture capital came from Europe, and profitability was based on overseas markets. All sugar plantations and plantation economies (the southern United States, the Caribbean islands, the north coast of South America, and Brazil) competed with one another for shares of a world market

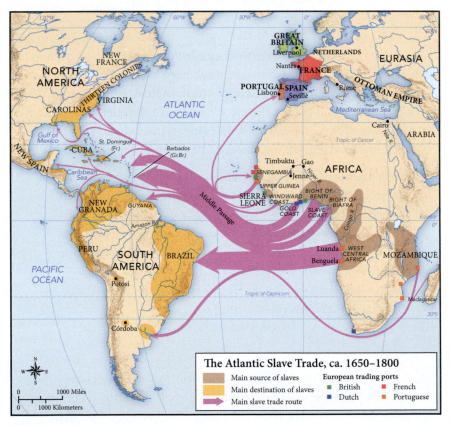

The Atlantic Slave Trade, ca. 1650–1800

Main source of slaves
Main destination of slaves
Main slave trade route

European trading ports
British   French
Dutch   Portuguese

Map 5.1

in sugar. The owners in each country worried that that natural advantages of climate and transportation favored a competitor, who would undercut prices. A natural disaster or political upheaval could make a whole island no longer competitive but provide boom conditions for other producers. Overproduction and price crashes were chronic.[12]

At a scale smaller than Gunder Frank's vast economic world system, important differences emerge between slavery in the United States and slavery in the Caribbean. First, virtually all of the owners of Caribbean sugar plantations were absentees. The colonizing country controlled currency, banking, and credit. Plantations were a way of making money, rather like owning a mine. In contrast, plantations in the United States primarily supported the elegant lifestyle of their owners.[13] Second, the number of whites in the Caribbean, perhaps 10 percent, was much lower than in the United States, where more than 50 percent of the population was white. In the southern United States many whites were small farmers, selling produce to nearby towns. Though Esteban mentions some small farmers in Cuba, there was nothing like the number found in the southern United States. His memoir suggests, however, that town folk in Cuba depended for food on the small plots cultivated by enslaved people:

> Almost all of them [the slaves] had little strips of land to be sown close
> to the barraccoons, almost behind them. Everything grew there: sweet
> potatoes, gourds, okra, kidney beans, which were like lima beans, yucca
> and peanuts. They also raised pigs. And they sold all these products to
> the whites who came out from the villages.[14]

Third, slaves born in the Caribbean formed a larger percentage of plantation workers than in the southern United States, where most slaves came from Africa.

Regional contrasts within the Caribbean are also striking. In some places slaves could choose their mate and marry. In others they could not. In some islands slaves had some standing, if minimal, in court. In others locations, they had absolutely no access to courts. In some places, like Esteban's plantation, slaves could cultivate small plots, sell their produce, and keep the money. Other islands permitted none of this. Contrasts between the Caribbean and mainland South America are even greater. In Peru, for example, the steep terrain did not permit large-scale plantations. The countryside was dotted with smallholdings, usually terraced plots. Slavery did appear in Peru during Spanish times, but slaves served in houses, small fields, construction, and ranching. Overall, when we try to describe "slavery," we must answer the questions of exactly where and when. To a slave, small day-to-day freedoms, though minimal, could make the difference between survival and complete despair.[15]

Factions, Beliefs, and Strategies for Survival

As Esteban observed, enslaved people carried their original religious beliefs and practices, although Catholicism increasingly influenced or even replaced traditional religions:

> A *nganga*, or a large pot, was placed in the center of the patio. The powers were inside the pot: the saints. People started drumming and singing. They took offerings to the pot and asked for health for themselves and their brothers and peace among themselves. They also made *enkangues*, which were charms of earth from the cemetery; the earth was made into little heaps in four corners, representing the points of the universe. Inside the pot they put a plant called star-shake, together with corn-straw to protect the men. When the master punished a slave, the others would collect a little earth and put it in the pot. With the help of this earth they could make the master fall sick or bring some harm upon his family, for so long as the earth was inside the pot the master was imprisoned there and the Devil himself couldn't get him out. That was how the Congolese revenged themselves on the master.[16]

Esteban noticed the fault lines and factions on the plantation. Congolese (from the interior of Africa) did not like West Africans and had separate shamans, who in turn competed with Catholic priests for followers. Esteban says that only house slaves—pampered softies in the eyes of field slaves—took up Catholicism.

> The household slaves were given rewards by their masters, and I never saw one of them badly punished. When they were ordered to go to the fields to cut cane or tend to the pigs, they would pretend to be ill so that they needn't work. For this reason the field slaves could not stand the sight of them. The household slaves sometimes came to the barracoons to visit relatives and take back fruit and vegetables for the master's house. . . . They caused a lot of trouble in the barracoons. The men came and tried to take liberties with the women. That was the source of the worst tensions. I was about twelve then, and I saw the whole rumpus.[17]

Esteban is unsparing in his descriptions of the brutal punishments that slaves endured:

> I saw many horrors in the way of punishment under slavery. That is why I didn't like the life. The stocks, which were in the boiler-house, were the cruelest. Some were for standing and others for lying down.

2.º Partie.   PL. 29.

J.B.Debret et la V.ᵉ de Portes del.ᵗ   Lith. de Thierry Frères, Sⁿ d'Engelmann & Cⁱᵉ

BOUTIQUE DE CORDONNIER.

A white shoemaker beats one of his slaves with a wooden paddle, Brazil. c. 1825.

They were made of thick planks with holes for the head, hands and feet. They would keep slaves fastened up like this for two or three months for some trivial offence. . . . The most common punishment was flogging; this was given by the overseer with a rawhide lash which made weals on the skin. They also had whips made of fibers from some jungle plant which stung like the devil and flayed off the skin in strips. I saw many handsome big Negroes with raw backs. Afterwards the cuts were covered with compresses of tobacco leaves, urine and salt.[18]

Part of a strategy for survival was to take small pleasures despite a twelve-hour workday and a six-day workweek:

Strange as it may seem, the Negroes were able to keep themselves amused in the barracoons. They had their games and pastimes. . . . The favorite game in the barracoons was *tejo*. A split corn-cob was placed on the ground with a coin balanced on top, a line drawn not far off, and you had to throw a stone from there to hit the cob. If the stone hit the cob so that the coin fell on top of it, the player won the coin, but if it fell nearby, he didn't. This game gave rise to great disputes, and then you had to take a straw to measure whether the coin was nearer the player or the cob.[19]

There were also fiestas on Sunday, the only nonwork day:

> Sunday was the liveliest day in the plantations. I don't know where the slaves found the energy for it. Their biggest fiestas were held on that day. On some plantations the drumming started at midday or one o'clock. At Flora de Sagua it began very early. The excitement, the games, and the children rushing around started at sunrise. The barracoon came to life in a flash; it was like the end of the world. And in spite of work and everything the people woke up cheerful. . . . Everyone had a special outfit for that day. The Negroes bought themselves rawhide boots, in a style I haven't seen since, from nearby shops where they went with the master's permission. They wore red and green *vayajá* scarves around their necks, and round their heads and waists, too, like in the *mani* dance. . . . The *yuka* was danced in couples, with wild movements. Sometime they swooped about like birds, and it almost looked as if they were going to fly, they moved so fast. They gave little hops with their hands on their waists. Everyone sang to excite the dancers. . . . The slaves of French descent danced in pairs, not touching, circling slowly around. If one of them danced outstandingly well they tied silk scarves of all colours to his knees as a prize. They sang in patois and played two big drums with their hands. This was called the French dance.[20]

Esteban's Life as a Runaway

Esteban's overall judgment on plantation slavery was clear: "Life was hard and bodies wore out. Anyone who did not take to the hills as a runaway when he was young had to become a slave. It was preferable to be on your own on the loose than locked up in all that dirt and rottenness."[21] His first attempt to escape failed and he spent time shackled in the stocks. But Esteban never doubted that he would run away again:

> I have never forgotten the first time I tried to escape. That time I failed, and I stayed a slave for several years longer for fear of having the

shackles put on me again. But I had the spirit of a runaway watching over me, which never left me. And I kept my plans to myself so that no one could give me away.... There were few runaways. People were afraid of the forest. They said that anyone who ran away was bound to be recaptured.[22]

Esteban made it to the forest and eluded capture. He lived in a secret cave with thousands of bats for a year and a half, staying alive by seizing roaming pigs at a marsh near the cave and stealing vegetables from white-owned small farms. After he left the cave, he walked forest paths, always alone:

> To tell the truth, I lived very well as a runaway, hidden but comfortable. I did not let other runaways catch sight of me; "Runaway meets runaway, sells runaway." ... I liked this solitude. The other runaways always stayed in groups of twos or threes, but this was dangerous because when it rained their footprints showed up in the mud, and lots of idiots were caught that way.[23]

He cured his illnesses with herbs from the forest. He seems to have spent about four years as a runaway slave, or *maroon* (from the Spanish term *cimmarón*, meaning "wild" or "untamed"). Esteban left the forest in 1886, when Spain abolished slavery. He was twenty-six years old.

Abolition and Rebellion

Let us turn from Esteban's story to the larger issue of the legal abolition of slavery. By 1500 northwest Europe—England, France, the Netherlands, and the principalities of Germany—was a zone with very few slaves. Even serfdom (labor bound to an estate, with many additional obligations to the lord of the manor) had largely disappeared. The decline started earlier but accelerated with the Black Death of the fourteenth century, a catastrophic outbreak of bubonic plague that spread from the Black Sea to Europe, the Middle East, and North Africa. Killing a third or more of the population in afflicted areas, the Black Death made labor more scarce and valuable. Attempts by the landed aristocrats to impose more rigorous conditions were often met with peasant rebellions. Despite the rise in the value of agricultural laborers, contract labor was generally cheaper than the maintenance of estate-bound serfs for a head of a manor in a developing cash-based economy. Too, land enclosure—the movement to larger, more efficient fields—made the long, narrow strips cultivated by serfs impractical. Like their Italian and Iberian counterparts, however, traders from northwest Europe continued to buy and sell slaves, just not within northwest Europe. English and Dutch slavers grew rich on the trade. Several centuries later it was in this relatively small nonslaveholding—but slave-trading—zone of northwest Europe that a movement for the abolition of slavery began.

Only once in human history have men and women mounted a sustained moral and political movement that rejected slavery and demanded its abolition in all societies. It managed to turn universal acceptance of slavery into universal condemnation in roughly 150 years, from 1770 to 1920. The abolition movement has been the subject of vast amounts of scholarly study and is worthy of more. By 1800 in England, the idea that England was a "free" country met with broad public support. In practice, thousands of free blacks lived in England, and no slaveholder from the colonies who arrived with slaves was willing to test his rights over his slaves by publicly whipping them or using them to pay debts, a legal right taken for granted in the American colonies.

In eighteenth-century France a myth gained popularity that the country had always been free. This image of French "freedom" rested uneasily with the reality of thousands of slaves in the French plantation colonies. From the 1720s to the 1790s, a few slaves from the colonies successfully challenged their master's right to hold slaves on French soil. The courts slowly established a boundary line for slaves. There was to be no slavery in France, but slavery was legal in the colonies, such as Haiti.[24] Secular political philosophers challenged this position in pre–French Revolution discussions of the inalienable rights of all people, including enslaved people.

In the eighteenth and the early nineteenth centuries, Europeans and American colonists could no longer ignore the slavery issue. Waves of slave rebellions in the colonies required costly military expeditions to suppress them. Slaves in the colonies fled to remote areas to form independent maroon settlements. Much scholarly literature has treated the various slave rebellions in the Caribbean and North and South America as isolated responses to local conditions. Recent research has convincingly argued the contrary, that the local conditions that triggered rebellions were, in fact, part of a larger competition among various European rivals (notably Holland, Great Britain, and France). European indentured, or contracted, laborers in the colonies, who felt as oppressed as the slaves, occasionally joined rebellions. The most famous slave rebellions were the successful revolution in Haiti (1791–1804) and the doomed Nat Turner's Rebellion in Virginia (1831), but literally hundreds of slave revolts broke out from Brazil to the southern United States. The earliest coincided with the beginnings of the transatlantic slave trade and ended only with slavery's abolition in the nineteenth century.[25]

Map 5.3

In the nineteenth century the secular and religious wings of the abolition movement lobbied, generally successfully, for laws in various countries that banned first the slave trade and then slavery itself. The earliest such laws appeared in Denmark, Great Britain, and France, followed by other countries in Europe, then Russia. Russian conquest of the Caucasus in the 1820s largely ended its slave trade with the nearby Ottoman and Safavid empires. Later in the nineteenth century slavery was banned in the European colonies of Asia and the Caribbean. Revolutions settled the issue in some South and Central American colonies, but emancipation was patchy through the nineteenth century. The Civil War and the Emancipation Proclamation ended slavery in in the United States. The last areas to ban slavery were Brazil, the princely states of India, some countries that emerged from the defeated Ottoman Empire after World War I, Ethiopia, and various kingdoms within the European-dominated colonies of sub-Saharan Africa.

The End of Slavery in Cuba

LIBERTY.

THE SHADOW OF ENGLISH LIBERTY IN AMERICA.

"The Shadow of English Liberty in America."
Satirical cartoon, *Punch Magazine*, 1850.

We left Esteban coming out of the forest after Spain abolished slavery in its colonies. No longer a fugitive, he sought employment on a sugar plantation. It was back to the barracoons, but with important changes. Even though the workers had a 9:00 p.m. curfew, there were no locks on the door, better air circulation (because the workers had knocked holes in the walls), improved food, twenty-five pesos a month pay, and the right to leave if the owner resorted to whipping. On Esteban's plantation the day-to-day violence had ended, but government violence remained. The governor of the province where Esteban's plantation was located was a brutal, sadistic official:

> Once he hit on the idea of sending Negros to the island of Fernando Poo, a terrible punishment because it was a desert island, a place of crocodiles and sharks. They let the Negroes loose there, and there was no way to escape. Thieves, pimps, cattle-rustlers were all sent there, and anyone with a tattoo mark, because tattoos were said to be a sign of rebellion against the Spanish government.[26]

The ethnic mix of workers remained about the same. The Congolese were the majority, in addition to Filipinos, Chinese, Canary Islanders, and "increasing number of Creoles," that is, men and women born in the islands and of mixed ethnic parentage.[27] Esteban spent about eighteen years in this "free" life on plantations. He saw men with more relative freedom than he had. A man would contract with a plantation owner to clear and prepare a section of land at a fixed price per square yard; he was free to move on to another plantation when the work was done. Esteban's memoir noted the technological changes on the larger and more modern plantations. Steam power ground the cane and crushed it to extract the juice. It also ran the mixer, a big machine that ground up the raw sugar after boiling down the juice. Steam also powered the centrifuges, which extracted the refined sugar from the thick sludge.

Cuba's Revolutions

Cuba first rebelled against Spain in 1868. Eight years old at the time, Esteban remembered nothing about the uprising, although he certainly heard stories about it in the decades that followed. In Cuba's second rebellion he was wholly involved. Fully one-third of Esteban's memoir is devoted to his struggles in the revolution against Spain between 1895 and 1898. It was a chaotic and violent time. Esteban and men from his plantation joined the rebels. No one had a gun, but they all had their machetes for cutting sugar cane:

> I joined the war on the third or fourth of December, 1895. I was at Ariosa [a plantation] still, but keeping informed of everything. One day I got together with some friends, the oldest people on the plantation, and I told them we ought to pluck up courage and join properly. The first person to follow my example was Juan Fabregas, a bold resolute Negro. I hardly had to tell him anything; he guessed what I was planning to do. We left the plantation in the evening and walked til we got to a farm, where we took the first horses we came across, tethered to a tree. This wasn't stealing, because I took care to ask the farmer for them properly. "Please be so kind as to give me a saddle," which he did, and I put it straight on the horse with reins and spurs. I had everything I needed to go to war, I had no fire-arms, but a machete was enough for those days. . . . When I came across the rebel forces I shouted to them, and they turned and saw me and the men with me. From that day onwards I gave myself wholly to the war. I felt a bit strange at first.[28]

Esteban says that some rebel leaders were merely thugs and bandits, interested only in pillaging the countryside. Other leaders successfully attacked Spanish troops, who responded with great cruelty to rebels and civilians. Esteban ends his memoir in 1905 with the United States militarily dominating Cuba. He saw the American domination as much preferable to Cuba as a Spanish colony He lived long enough, however, to witness Communist leader Fidel Castro's successful revolution against US control of Cuba (1953–1959). Even at 105, Esteben offered his machete "anytime" his country was threatened.

Insurgents attack a Spanish supply train in the Revolution of 1868.

The Bigger Picture

Modern Slavery

Significant differences exist between slavery in the world before abolition and slavery today. Then, it was legal, accepted, and widely practiced. Peoples around the world successfully asserted that slavery was part of their culture. They also claimed that slave trade and ownership were essential elements of their economies. With the abolition movement and changing economic and political conditions, "old" slavery declined in the late nineteenth and early twentieth centuries. Slaveholding societies such as the southern United States, the Ottoman Empire, Egypt, and North Africa shifted to other forms of labor, though conditions for many former slaves improved little. Today slavery is illegal in all countries of the world and is generally considered immoral and a violation of human rights. Nations can no longer plausibly claim that slavery is purely a matter of "internal policy." Today a series of international agreements and United Nations statements define a person's basic freedoms anywhere in the world. These documents are supplemented by specific legal statements, which identify the rights of children and of women and condemn the enslavement of people across international borders. Mechanisms are in place to initiate international economic sanctions to punish states that countenance slavery within their borders.

The Endurance of Slavery

These shifts in societal attitudes, national laws, and international agreements should have meant the end of slavery, but they did not. Several forms of slavery continue to taint our world, such as the exploitation of children. In many Asian, African, and South American countries, children must work to help poor families survive. This practice shades into slavery when a family, so destitute that it cannot feed or take care of its children, gives a daughter as unpaid domestic labor to a wealthier family or relative. In a similar route to slavery, a slaver promises the poor and desperate family that the child will be adopted by a rich family in a wealthy country and have a much better life. This scenario is only rarely true—typically the children end up as domestic slaves. When the girls should be in school, they are instead washing laundry, carrying water, preparing food, and cleaning the house. They are unpaid and kept silenced through implied and actual violence. Child labor, of both boys and girls, weaves many of the carpets sold across the world. Children work in slave conditions in the mines in South America. The children should be in school, but they work the entire day.

In 1956, at a convention on the abolition of slavery, the United Nations explicitly condemned dowry, that is, a transaction in which a "woman, without the right to refuse, is promised or given in marriage on payment of a consideration in money or in kind to her

A young child breaks bricks in Bangladesh, 2020.

parents, guardian, family or any other person or group."[29] If, as many would argue, dowry is, indeed, a form of slavery, it is one of the most prevalent forms of slavery in the modern world. Dowry negotiations are typical in India and across much of Asia, the Middle East, and Africa. In India, dowry is completely open and public with expectations published in newspapers. Various initiatives by government and voluntary organizations have failed to stop it. If anything, middle-class dowries have gone up in recent decades.

In the twentieth century, certain states, for example, Nazi Germany, pursued slavery as public policy. By 1941, the regime impressed as slave labor more than 3 million men and women from lands overrun by the German army. In the same year, Germany repudiated the provision in the Geneva Conventions, the core of international humanitarian law, against the use of captured soldiers or civilians as slave labor and devised a plan for the creation of 12,000 labor camps for the permanent enslavement of Slavs. For Jews and ethnicities designated as "expendable," the Nazi labor camps were intended to kill, not just to provide labor. This policy of "work to death" spread to captured Russians in the German munitions works. By 1944, foreign, conscripted slave labor reached 7 million, deployed in camps, in factories, and on farms.

The Nazis viewed slavery as a long-term strategy. Their plans included more than 12 million slaves for postwar construction projects. Albert Speer, Hitler's Minister of War Production, envisioned that Nazi Germany and its occupied lands would emerge from World War II as a permanent slave state.

The Nazis were far from alone in turning their own citizens into state slaves. In the Soviet Union, from the 1930s to the mid-1950s millions of dissidents, teachers, peasants resisting collectivization (the replacement of individual farms with large communal ones run by the state), ethnic groups, and religious minorities disappeared into forced-labor camps. Under Stalin, nearly 2 million people were swept up in 1938 alone. Prisoners captured in World War II likewise entered the system, many held for years after the end of the war. Slave labor first built the camps, then railroads and roads in the harsh, cold north. Larger in scale than the use of slavery by either Hitler or Stalin was Mao Zedong's use of slavery in China. The state used forced-labor camps and enslavement in the countryside over decades as punishment for anyone perceived as a threat to the Communist Party: businessmen, relatively wealthy peasants, teachers, students, and owners of property. Modern scholars have estimated that more than 20 million prisoners passed through some form of slavery in China in the second half of the twentieth century.

The New Slavery
In the past decades, large-scale changes across the world have made possible a new form of slavery. First, the poor became poorer with fewer opportunities. The human population expanded as never before, just as common agricultural land became privately owned. The poor found it increasingly difficult to supplement what food they grew with food gathered from shrinking, jointly held grazing and forest land. Illiteracy remained high in

villages. Second, new transportation links connected previously remote areas to growing cities. What once might have been a four-month caravan trip became a four-hour airplane trip. Transporting slaves became much cheaper and easier. Third, war, often between regions or ethnic groups, became endemic, creating refugees and permanent refugee camps. Slavery today, then, is a result of serious, complex, overlapping social problems that include poverty and landlessness, illiteracy, gender discrimination, ethnic and religious discrimination, dysfunctional families, and endemic warfare. Slavery is often an outcome of some combination of these social problems.[30]

As in earlier times, there are no "typical" slaves and there is no "typical" slavery. Patterns vary by region of supply, transport networks, and the eventual situation of the enslaved. Slavery remains immoral and illegal, but like other high-risk, high-return businesses, opportunities for huge profits can make slavery attractive to unscrupulous criminal networks. Smuggling of slaves often overlaps with smuggling of drugs, cigarettes, alcohol, and arms.

In one pattern of modern-day slavery, in a low-wage country with high unemployment, such as Thailand or Azerbaijan, a recruiter—often a fashionably dressed woman—offers rural women high-paying overseas jobs in tourism or entertainment. When the women arrive in the new country, slavers seize their papers and force them into prostitution. Fake marriage brokers also serve the sex trade and domestic bondage. Women in Nepal or rural China receive offers of marriage from desirable-sounding men, who apparently have good jobs and houses. The women arrive expecting to be brides, and are in fact forced into prostitution. Men in areas of high unemployment are also subject to similar slaving operations. They are lured with promises of factory jobs with good wages only to be enslaved into hard, dangerous, unpaid work after they arrive.

On the personal level, the costs of slavery are enormous: physical damage, decreased health, depression and other mental problems, loss of innocence, even rejection by one's family. In sex slavery, even if the woman manages to escape and is repatriated to her home country, often she cannot find work, just as there was no work available before she fell into slavery. In many cultures she is a shame and dishonor to the family and unmarriageable, since many men have sexually used her. Retrafficking is frequent.

At the societal level, slavery corrupts the region where the slaves came from. It undermines families—both nuclear and extended—and marriage patterns. It supports organized crime and subjugates young people who might demand change. Slavery also corrodes the location receiving the slaves. It undercuts free labor, funds organized crime and political corruption, and fosters the development of a culture of guns and violence. Slavery undermines public safety when unscrupulous police accept bribes and come to see the slavers as their "clients" rather than all citizens as their employers.

What Is to Be Done?
Beyond declarations and resolutions, what can be done to help end modern-day slavery? Initiatives are possible at the personal level, in businesses and industries, and at the

national and international level. At the personal level, we all have the right and obligation to ask whether slavery or any form of exploitation is embedded in any product we buy. For example, an organization known as Rugmark offers third-party certification that handmade rugs from Asia are not made by slaves or children. The certification is common in Europe and spreading to the United States. Sellers of Fair Trade Coffee also certify that no workers in the coffee's cultivation and processing are slaves or ill paid. We also have the obligation to publicize any information on slavery that we find. The internet makes this simple and inexpensive. We also can read the government reports of slavery and efforts to eradicate it. Especially important is the annual *Trafficking in Persons Report* from the US State Department. We can also support programs and organizations that oppose slavery through publicity, education, and local job opportunities, especially in rural areas.

At the national level, we can encourage our government to prosecute slavers aggressively and to pressure weak or unwilling countries to do the same. We can support foreign aid that is premised on a country's efforts to decrease slavery within its borders. Government programs to decrease rural poverty will help and should be supported. At the international level, Free the Slaves is an international NGO (nongovernmental organization). We can turn to its website, www.freetheslaves.net, to discover how each of us can play a role in supporting efforts to free the enslaved and to dismantle some of the systems that allow slavery to exist.

TIMELINE

ca. 1500
Slavery is largely absent from northwestern Europe,

ca. 1720–ca. 1790
Slaves from France's colonies successfully challenge their masters' right to hold slaves on French soil

ca. 1770
Beginning of abolition movement

1791–1804
Haitian Revolution

1800
Idea of England as a "free" country gains public support

1831
Nat Turner's Rebellion in Virginia

1860
Esteban Montejo is born into slavery, in the Spanish colony of Cuba

1868
Cuba rebels against Spain

1870
Esteban works as a driver of a bagasse wagon, transporting sugarcane.

ca. 1882–1886
Esteban lives in the forest as a runaway slave (maroon)

The scholar and human rights activist Christien van den Anker has suggested five principles that should underlay any action to suppress modern slavery. In brief, she calls for:

1. Respect for the rights of the victims.
2. Justice for all as the basis for policies and laws.
3. Respect for the ability of slaves to define their situation.
4. Changes in global business to promote equality between producers and consumers.
5. Development of viable alternative livelihoods, especially in poor rural areas.[31]

These principles form a means for all of us to think about the problem of slavery and how we might, at last, eliminate it.

For digital learning resources, please go to
www.oup.com/he/gordon-seventhemes1e

1886
Slavery is abolished in Cuba, and Esteban leaves the forest

1886–ca. 1904
Esteban works as a free man on Cuban plantations

1895–1898
Esteban joins rebels in revolution against Spain

1905
United States seizes power over Cuba

ca. 1930–1955
Millions disappear into forced labor camps in the Soviet Union

1941–1944
Rise of slave labor as public policy in Nazi Germany

ca. 1950–2000
20 million prisoners pass through some form of slavery in China

1953–1959
Fidel Castro's revolution against US control of Cuba

1956
United Nations explicitly condemns the practice of dowry

1965
Montejo tells stories of his life to anthropologist Miguel Barnet

Human Rights

The Big Picture: Defining Human Rights

The violation of human rights is today one of the most serious accusations possible to level against an individual, a group, or a government. It might seem self-evident that ethnic cleansing—the mass expulsion or killing of members of an unwanted ethnic or religious group—as well as slavery, the jailing of journalists, and the execution of prisoners without trial constitute high crimes and deserve severe punishment. The history and practice of recognizing and defining human rights is, however, far from straightforward.

For centuries, even millennia, the definition of a moral life was fragmented. Each religion defined moral and immoral acts for its followers, and kings promulgated codes of moral behavior within their kingdom. People beyond the kingdom's boundaries or outside a religion were at best tolerated with limited rights or, more commonly, treated as aliens to be hated and feared. This sort of thinking has produced some of humankind's most heinous events, such as the massacre of Huguenots (French Protestants) in sixteenth- and seventeenth-century France and, in our own time, the expulsion and slaughter of Muslims in the predominantly Buddhist country of Myanmar (formerly Burma).

Groundbreaking research by historian Lynn Hunt argues that to understand the history and development of human rights we need not analyze every philosophical or legal writing across the world that touches on rights. All of these statements and judgments, while

> **Protesters demonstrate against the mass killings of the Rohingya people by the government of Myanmar, 2015.**

interesting, do not form some sort of unified background that made inevitable the eventual statement of universal human rights. Hunt contends that the relevant ideas and formulations of human rights arose from profound changes in the perception of self in Europe and the American colonies in two short periods, one in the mid-eighteenth century and one at the century's end.[1] The eighteenth century was the "Age of Enlightenment" in the West, a period of unprecedented optimism in the potential of knowledge and reason to understand and change the world. Enlightenment scholars argued that the exercise of disciplined reason was the key to truth and progress. While this view was largely validated—most dramatically in the field of science—many Western thinkers wondered whether reason alone was sufficient. In the late eighteenth century the strictly rational approach of the Enlightenment came to be rivaled by a worldview emphasizing that emotion was the key to truth. This worldview, known as Romanticism, flourished in both art and literature.

Whether focused on reason or emotion, both the Enlightenment and Romanticism celebrated the self. One marker of these changes in the perception of self was, for example, the appearance of a new type of novel in England and France that placed the reader directly inside the sufferings and triumphs of the central character, typically a woman. Novels such as Samuel Richardson's *Pamela* (1740) and Jean-Jacques Rousseau's *Julie,*

The Romantic ideal: *Two Men Contemplating the Moon* **by Casper David Friedrich, 1819.**

or the New Heloise (1761) were immensely popular, widely distributed, and translated into the main European languages. If women had an interior self not controlled by a father, brother, or a husband, was not she a full, independent person entitled to all the "rights of man"? The implications of declaring universal rights in both the French (1789–1799) and the American (1775–1781) revolutions raised bold questions about those largely or wholly without rights, such as women, children, foreigners, slaves, and men without property. These issues were—in the most literal sense—fought over for country-by-country for decades. The US Civil War, for example, must be seen in the context of such struggles.

Today's acceptance of human rights constitutes a new understanding of humanity and what it means to be human. Human rights accrue to all people on the planet by their very existence as human beings. As a moral code, human rights do not depend on belonging to a religion or holding citizenship in a particular state. Yet as the example of Muslims in Myanmar shows, the promulgation of human rights has been entangled with power politics on a global scale, existing religions, self-identified cultures, minority peoples, and the end of European empires.[2] Despite these difficulties, human rights offers a framework to identify and deal with ethnic conflict, gender discrimination, even state-sponsored mass incarceration. The most central statement of human rights remains the *Universal Declaration of Human Rights* (1948), formulated in the aftermath of World War II and within the structure of the newly constituted United Nations. This document is one of the most important foundational statements of the modern world. The drafting committee's discussions, references to earlier events and thinkers, and compromises are essential for our understanding of it.

Our guide to the drafting of the Universal Declaration of Human rights is Eleanor Roosevelt. She was the widow of President Franklin Delano Roosevelt, who had guided the United States through the Great Depression of the 1930s and World War II (1937–1945), and in her own right a tireless fighter for women's rights, labor rights, and social and economic assistance to the poor and refugees. Fortunately, much of her correspondence from the period remains, as do memoirs of the participants and verbatim records of some of the official discussions of human rights. These records contain vivid interchanges revealing how the delegates struggled with visions of a better

Eleanor Roosevelt making a radio speech, 1944.

future: what it meant to be human, how governments should treat their citizens, how men should treat women, how companies should treat their workers, and how wars should be conducted. Was it possible for an international organization to enforce equal pay for equal work? Was it possible for a statement of human rights to address disparities in wages around the world? Could refugees become citizens of the world rather than people lacking citizenship? Could an international organization end child slavery? Could people of good will articulate human rights for everyone?

From World War to Human Rights

As World War II drew to a close, people across the globe anticipated a new international order, but there was precious little consensus on what it would be. Great Britain did not want other nations insisting it free its worldwide colonies or set the terms or proclaim a timetable for decolonization. The Soviet Union wanted acceptance of its dominance of Eastern Europe and recognition of a de facto border between Eastern and Western Europe. The United States wanted prosecution of Nazi war criminals but also support for rebuilding Germany. Less powerful states, such as Australia and especially South and Central American countries, wanted protections from postwar economic domination by the United States. Charitable organizations pushed for rules for humane treatment of prisoners and civilians during war, better refugee treatment, and peacetime protections for citizens from oppression by their own governments. Labor unions wanted a United Nations committed to worker rights and economic justice. Everyone hoped for a better world, which might at least in part justify the horrendous death and suffering of the Second World War.

Competing interests rapidly emerged during the drafting of the United Nations charter in San Francisco in 1945. The delegates of the fifty participant Allied nations met only ten times, but the various committees and subcommittees met over 400 times. Human rights received a prominent position in the preamble to the charter as one of the principal justifications for the United Nations: "We the Peoples of the United Nations [are] determined...to reaffirm faith in fundamental human rights, in the dignity and worth of the human person, in the equal rights of men and women and of nations large and small."[3] The delegates well understood that the drafting of the United Nations charter was fraught with problems, but they also saw the charter as a great hope for peace and a better future.

Two immediate problems plagued human rights as featured in the UN charter. First, human rights were not defined; this vagueness allowed delegations (such as those from the USSR, Yugoslavia, and Saudi Arabia) to support the formation of the United Nations despite their reservations about human rights. Second, the

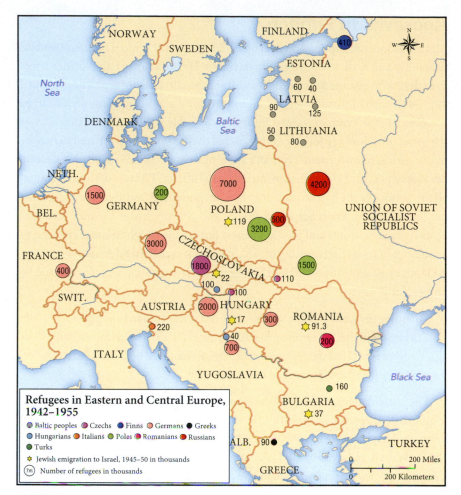

Map 6.1

charter prominently stated that the United Nations would not meddle in the internal affairs of members, no matter how much a government abused its citizens: "Nothing contained in the present Charter shall authorize the United Nations to intervene in matters which are essentially within the domestic jurisdiction of any state."[4] Late in the talks on the charter, smaller states managed to include economic and social issues as an important part of the United Nations' work with a charge to establish a commission to monitor conditions and suggest improvements.

The translation from vague aspirations to a clear statement of universal human rights awaited a functional organizational structure for the United Nations, which came together in the second half of 1945. There would be six "commissions" or "councils," each with a staff and charged with one of the major activities of the organization. Human rights fell under the Economic and Social Commission.

Roosevelt in London

Eleanor Roosevelt's appointment as a US delegate to the United Nations General Assembly had little to do with human rights. Harry Truman, the former Vice-President who assumed the presidency after Franklin D. Roosevelt's death (April 12, 1945), wished to maintain as much continuity and association with FDR as possible. Hence Truman wanted Eleanor in a visible public role. Eleanor was, at the same time, looking for something useful to do, though she refused to run for public office. She accepted Truman's appointment to the US delegation despite her lack of practical experience in international affairs. The rest of the delegation, all men, thought she had no place in serious negotiations and vigorously opposed her appointment. With her usual energy and thoroughness Eleanor read and absorbed the briefings and position papers during the rough Atlantic crossing to London, where the first meeting of the United Nations General Assembly opened on January 10, 1946. She worried that she would fail and that her failure would be far-reaching:

> During the entire London session of the Assembly I walked on eggs.
> I knew as the only woman on the delegation I was not very welcome.
> Moreover, if I failed to be a useful member, it would not be considered a
> chance for others to serve in the near future.[5]

The male American delegates assigned Eleanor to the Economic and Social Commission, assuming that little of importance would happen there. They could not have been more wrong. Within days it was clear that refugee rights was one of the most divisive issues of the London meeting. The United States wanted free movement of the millions of refugees to places where they could find better lives. The Soviet Union expected to force refugees to return to their country of origin regardless of the treatment they would receive. With millions of lives at stake, Eleanor Roosevelt delivered a powerful, well-reasoned statement of the American position, rebutting the Soviet argument as presented by the Deputy Foreign Minister. With this speech she won over her own delegation, who at the end of the London meeting told her, "We found you good to work with. And we will be happy to do so again."[6]

The Universal Declaration of Human Rights: The Long Road to Passage

Shortly after Eleanor's return to New York City (site of UN headquarters), the Economic and Social Council of the United Nations asked her to sit on its permanent Committee on Human Rights, and she accepted. In the following months,

Ukrainian refugees near the city of Sevastopol in the Crimean Peninsula, April 1944.

it became clear that time was short for the United Nations to draft any statement of human rights. Both the USSR and the United States were hardening their rivalry, and "peaceful coexistence" seemed less and less likely. Many predicted a nuclear World War III within a year. Members of the newly formed Human Rights Commission elected Eleanor Roosevelt as its chair in April 1946.

Over the next few months, proposals about human rights inundated both the Human Rights Commission and its oversight committee, the Economic and Social Council. At the fourth meeting of the US branch of the Human Rights Commission (held in May 1946 at New York City's Hunter College), Roosevelt reminded delegates of the seriousness of their job:

> I feel very strongly, judging by the letters that I am getting, that this
> Commission means a great deal to a great many people in the world . . . To
> the peoples of the world we have a very grave responsibility, because they
> look upon us as representatives of the peoples of the world. . . . and for that
> reason I hope that every one of us is going to feel a grave personal respon-
> sibility as well as naturally, a responsibility to represent what our govern-
> ments believe is right.[7]

The future of the UN Human Rights Commission did not seem promising. Only six of the nine delegates showed up for the first full meeting (January

27–February 19, 1947), and the Soviet Union sent a replacement delegate who explicitly disavowed all that his predecessor had agreed to or done. After an initial meeting of the drafting committee (lasting almost two weeks), the delegates produced only one proposal, that delegates should represent only themselves, not their government.[8] The Economic and Social Council summarily rejected this suggestion.

Months passed with no apparent progress, but the staff of the Economic and Social Council quietly considered and collated the many human-rights proposals received. Sniping between the United States and the USSR continued. The Soviets demanded a special subcommission on rights of minorities focused on the situation of blacks in the United States; the Americans demanded a subcommission on the freedom of journalists and the press.[9] Eleanor Roosevelt did a masterful, even-handed job of moving ahead on topics where agreement was possible. One advantage was that the full Commission on Human Rights had delegates from eighteen countries, most of which were not closely tied to the Soviet Union or the United States. Immediately after the meeting, Eleanor Roosevelt gave John Humphery, a forty-year-old Canadian law professor from McGill University, the task of creating a first draft of the statement of Human Rights. Delegates demanded a larger drafting committee, and eventually nine countries were represented.

Throughout the spring of 1947, Humphery and United Nations Secretariat staff read voluminous suggestions of individuals and nations. Lebanese philosopher and diplomat Charles Malik, one of the crucial members of the drafting committee, later wrote that the members felt "completely lost; we had no conception of how to proceed with the task entrusted to us."[10] They pushed on, preparing for a meeting of the full drafting committee in June 1947. Humphery and the staff produced an unwieldy list of forty-eight human rights, some of them adapted from earlier statements of rights, such as those from major religions, the French Revolution, and the American Revolution. Other rights on Humphery's list were drawn from the constitutions of various countries and communications from people and governments around the world. Political events looked bleaker than ever. The USSR actively supported Communist uprisings in Turkey and Greece. The United States adopted the Truman Doctrine, which stated that the nation would support "free peoples who are resisting subjugation by armed minorities or by outside pressures."[11] The United States shipped arms to anti-Communist fighters in Greece and Turkey.

Even with the Cold War between the United States and the Soviet Union heating up, the Economic and Social Council queried philosophers, statesmen, and moralists of the time on their conception of human rights. Letters came back from the civil-rights activist Mahatma Gandhi and the philosophers Pierre Teilhard

De Chardin and Benedetto Croce. Some replies focused on human rights in Chinese philosophy. Rights in Confucian thought came from notions of the good and just government with no mention of God. Rights in Islam came from the Qur'an and the sayings of the Prophet. The just Muslim state merged secular and religious authority. Rights in Hinduism were based on classical texts, which included the caste system. Jews had a clear idea of justice but it was for their community, not for outsiders. Non-Jews did not have standing in Jewish courts. Other replies discussed a possible biological basis for human rights, human rights in "primitive" societies, or science and human rights. Reconciling these disparate bases for human rights seemed impossible.

Jacques Maritain, a French philosopher who oversaw this project, was at first pessimistic about the possibility of any statement of universal rights. Deep examination of the rights of Roman citizens, Enlightenment philosophy, or the underpinnings of Islamic law would quickly become an endlessly contentious enterprise. Then Maritain noticed that across the world people's views on human rights were curiously similar despite their different philosophical or religious bases. His initial pessimism gave way to optimism about drafting a charter of universal human rights:

Jacque Maritain speaking in Rome, 1945.

> Where it is a question of rational interpretation and justifications of minds are not united in faith or philosophy, there will be mutual conflicts between interpretations and justifications. In the field of practical conclusions, on the other hand, agreement on a joint declaration is possible, given an approach pragmatic rather than theoretical in practice, however opposed the theoretical viewpoints.[12]

Informally, Maritain's ideas filtered into the discussions. The Brazilian representative proposed that the beginning of the preamble include "all human beings are created in the image and likeness of God."[13] The delegate from China reminded the group that Confucian ideals contained many human rights without any reference to an overarching God and that China constituted two-fifths of the of earth's population. The French delegate referenced Maritain's observation that rights could be agreed upon despite conflicting philosophies and religions. The Brazilian delegate dropped his amendment, and this was the last time that "God" was proposed in the drafting of the Declaration.

Eleanor Roosevelt holding the completed Declaration of Human Rights, 1949.

Finally, after nearly two years of often contentious discussion, layers of committees, and intensifying Cold War between the Soviet Union and the United States, the UN General Assembly passed the Universal Declaration of Human Rights on December 10, 1948. The vote was nearly unanimous, with only Saudia Arabia, the Soviet Union, and several Soviet client states abstaining. The Universal Declaration of Human Rights has now been in place for almost seventy-five years. It remains a document to be celebrated. For the first time in history, people came together to articulate not the rights of Canadians or Christians, Haitians or Hindus, but the rights belonging to every human being, solely on the basis of his or her humanity. The document asserts hopes and dreams for the freedoms, responsibilities, and living situations of all people in a jointly imagined future. It sets a standard and challenges governments, groups, and individuals to live up to it.

What Was Adopted

As passed by the UN General Assembly, the Universal Declaration of Human Rights consists of a preamble and thirty numbered paragraphs. It is written in everyday language, not legalese. The document has an internal logic reflected in its structure, perhaps best envisioned by René Cassin, a French delegate who served on the drafting committee from its first meeting to the final passage. He compared the Declaration to a classical Greek temple with a foundation, steps leading up to a pillared front, and a triangular pediment on top of the pillars.[14] The preamble was the foundation for the entire document (and for the imagined building). It asserts that each and every human being has inherent dignity and inalienable rights, which are the basis for freedom, justice, and peace in the world. People are entitled to freedom of speech and belief and freedom from fear and want, with their human rights protected by the rule of law. Relations between nations should be friendly. Men and women should have equal rights. Nations should be committed to social progress and better standards of life. In the Declaration, as laid out in the preamble, fundamental human rights are *recognized*, not *conferred*. They are not granted by a nation or subordinate to national rights. The Declaration is neither a treaty nor an international agreement; it states the rights of people all over the world.

Cassin visualized Articles 1 and 2 as the steps of the Greek temple, setting the tone of the remainder of the document. They stated that all human beings are born free and equal in dignity and rights, and each has conscience and reason. All people are entitled to the rights enumerated without distinction of race, color, sex, language, religion, political opinions, national origin, property, birth, or other status. This section of the Declaration especially emphasizes that everyone enjoys these rights regardless of political, jurisdictional, or international standing. It gives full rights to refugees and persons without country, as well as those in colonies.

On top of the steps are four pillars. On the left is a pillar representing Articles 3–11, concerned with personal rights, such as the right to life, liberty, and security. These nine articles forbid slavery, torture, and arbitrary detention. They assert everyone's right to be a "person" in courts of law, equal protection before the law, fair and public trials, and just tribunals to adjudicate violations of universal human rights. Everyone is to be presumed innocent until proven guilty. Laws cannot be enforced retroactively.

Moving right, the second pillar, Articles 12–17, focuses on the rights of people in civil society. All people should be free from arbitrary interference with family, home, or correspondence, and laws should support these rights. People should be able to move freely throughout a state and across international borders. Everyone has the right to a nationality and the right to change nationality. Every person of "full age" has the right to marry, but both parties must freely consent to the marriage. Laws should protect the family. Every person has the right to own property,

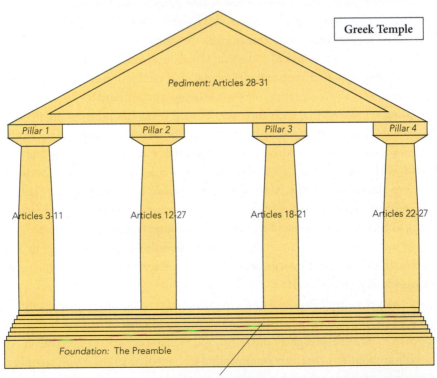

Greek Temple

Pediment: Articles 28-31

Pillar 1   Pillar 2   Pillar 3   Pillar 4

Articles 3-11   Articles 12-27   Articles 18-21   Articles 22-27

Foundation: The Preamble

Steps: Articles 1 and 2

Rene Cassin's Envisioning of the Universal Declaration of Human Rights as a Greek Temple

both alone and with others, and be free from arbitrary search and seizure. (Article 17 on property rights was fought over from the beginning of drafting to the final wording. The United States wanted a strong private-property ownership clause. The United Kingdom wanted no article at all, arguing that property law was already well established throughout the world. Latin American countries wanted a right to enough property to sustain a family. The USSR opposed the idea of sustenance based on private property rather than the state. The best the Commission could do was to eliminate the term "private" in association with property. No one was happy with the compromise, which limited the statement to vague generality.)

Continuing right, the next pillar represents Articles 18–21, concerned with freedom of religion and political belief. Each person has the right to freedom of thought, conscience, teaching, and worship, as well as the freedom to change religion. (This right was particularly opposed by conservative Muslim countries and was the basis of Saudi Arabia's abstention from the final General Assembly vote.) People should be free to express their opinion and receive information and ideas, regardless of frontiers. They have the right to peaceful assembly, and no state can require membership in any association. People have the right to participate in their government through elections and representation. Suffrage should be universal, equal, and by secret ballot. (The Soviet Union fiercely opposed these Articles, arguing that workers were entitled to rights precisely through associations and that elections were hollow bourgeois protections. Many countries with planned economies successfully resisted the US push to include the right to form political parties.)

The last pillar, on the far right, represents Articles 22–27, which describe an individual's social, economic, and cultural rights. These Articles lay out what a government should do for all its citizens. Work is indispensable for dignity. Therefore, everyone possesses a right to work, free choice of employment, and protection from unemployment. Equal pay for equal work is a universal human right. Everyone is entitled to just pay, enough to maintain the health of his or her family and to be secure in old age. The right to join labor unions is fundamental. Everyone has the right to rest periodically during the workday and enjoy holidays with pay. Turning from work, everyone has the right to education. Elementary education should be free and compulsory. All education should promote understanding, tolerance, and respect for all nations, races, and religious groups. (Article 26 is the only one that evoked Nazi Germany and the Holocaust, though indirectly.) Parents should be able to choose the manner of education for their children. Regarding cultural rights, everyone should be able to participate in the culture of his or her community, as well as share in scientific discoveries. Authors, scientists, and artists should benefit from their creations. (Article 25 would, indeed, affect many countries. It declared that all children, whether born in a marriage or out of wedlock, enjoyed the same protection and the same rights.)[15]

Atop the four pillars was what Cassin envisioned as the pediment, Articles 28–30, which focused on what would be required to bring these rights into reality in a civil society. Everyone has the right to live in a society that recognized the universal rights put forth in the Declaration. At the same time, all people had duties as well as rights: to support public order, morality, general welfare, and, as long as it supported peoples' universal rights, the legal system.

A Less Than Perfect Declaration

As we have seen, the delegates wrote, debated, and ultimately crafted the Universal Declaration of Human Rights against almost impossible odds. Worsening relations between the United States and the USSR put the drafting under tremendous time pressure. It is understandable that the document has gaps, overlapping assertions, internal contradictions, and vague language. Still, the Universal Declaration of Human Rights takes its place among other influential utopian documents that envision a desirable and honorable future.

Let us now turn to some of the problems of the Universal Declaration of Human Rights and their effects on the reach and effectiveness of the document.

First, there was no mechanism of action, no clear path, legal or otherwise, by which the United Nations could either push nations toward human rights or punish nations who violated human rights. Eleanor Roosevelt recognized that there would be considerable resistance to what was termed a "convention," that is, an agreement among nations on, in this case, a legal structure to enforce human rights and punish their violation. She knew, for example, that a convention would meet fierce opposition in the United States from Southern and conservative senators. Two dozen states enforced miscegenation laws (laws against racial mixing) at the time, which would have been blatantly unacceptable in the framework of human rights.[16] South Africa too was legislating severe apartheid and denial of human rights for blacks. It surely would have fought a convention. Within the United Nations it took years before there was an efficient means for declaring a human-rights emergency or deciding the proper course of action when a nation blatantly violated human rights. Not until 1966 did the United Nations establish a structure to adjudicate human-rights violations. The United States did not ratify this until 1992. During the so-called Arab Spring—a series of anti-government protests and rebellions that spread across much of the Middle East in the early 2010s—the collation of support for these popular uprisings against dictatorial rulers was largely done outside the United Nations.

Second, as we have seen, delegates opted for the individual, not the state, as the holder of human rights. Early on, in February 1947, the Lebanese diplomat Charles Malik laid out the "human rights as individual rights" position:

The human being is inherently prior to any group to which he may belong ... his mind and conscience are the most sacred and inviolable things about him, not his belonging to this or that class, this or that nation, or this or that religion. Any social pressure coming from whatever direction, be that his state or his religion, or his class, or any direction which determines his consent automatically is wrong ... the group to which he belongs, whatever it be, be it his state, or nation or anything, the group can be wrong, just as the individual can be wrong.[17]

Nevertheless, the Declaration recognized "stateism" at the insistence of the smaller countries and the Soviet Union. It is the state's obligation to provide economic and social security for the exercise of other human rights. Is it the state's duty to establish working conditions and length of workday? Implicitly the Declaration accepts state planning for the betterment of its citizens, which could (and did) cross the line from supporting human rights to subversion of human rights in favor of state control and planning.

Third, the relation of rights to duties and responsibilities was never spelled out in the Declaration. Rights were specified, but the attending responsibilities

Demonstration against apartheid in South Africa, 1964.

were not. Differences and tensions between the Soviet Union and the United States would not permit agreement.

Fourth, the issue of cultural rights has bedeviled adoption and enforcement of universal rights for decades. Did respect for cultural practices supersede the rights of persons within a culture to resist practices that violated universal human rights? For example, did the culture of the American South, which legally prohibited marriage between races, trump the right to marry as laid out in the Declaration? Did the established cultural practice of dowry take precedence over the Declaration's insistence on the right to marry without the woman being bought and sold? Did the Declaration's assertion of equality within marriage supersede Muslim marriage laws? Did the Declaration's assertion of the right to change religion without penalty supersede Islam's stern laws against apostasy?[18]

Fifth, there was no simple mechanism for deciding what is a human right and what is not. Instead, what should be added to the list of human rights or what should be subtracted from it is fought out in practical actions: strikes, demonstrations, elections, internal discussions within funding agencies, university courses, appeals to volunteers, and government legislation. The appeal of one claim or another necessarily varies from country to country and even among funding agencies within a single country.

Evolution of the Universal Declaration of Human Rights

Not long after the passage of the Universal Declaration of Human Rights by the UN General Assembly, Eleanor Roosevelt resigned as chair of the Commission on Human Rights. She felt that staying on would only exacerbate the hostility between the Soviet Union and the United States and that the position of chair needed to pass to a country less involved with the Cold War. In retrospect, she made the right decision. The Cold War would be fought with words and propaganda, blockades, and proxy wars, while nuclear bombs waited in the wings. The USSR used purges and show trials to keep its citizens loyal and angry at the United States. The United States did much the same with accusations that an unknown number of its citizens were Communists or Communist sympathizers. Emphasis on tolerance, camaraderie, and the primacy of universal rights faded into bleak confrontation and suspicion.

The Cold War was, however, not the only important feature of the world in the middle decades of the twentieth century. Protests and revolutions occurred in virtually every European colony, and many new states emerged. Between 1948, when the United Nations adopted the Universal Declaration of Human Rights, and 1965, sixty new countries replaced European colonies. Thirty-five of those

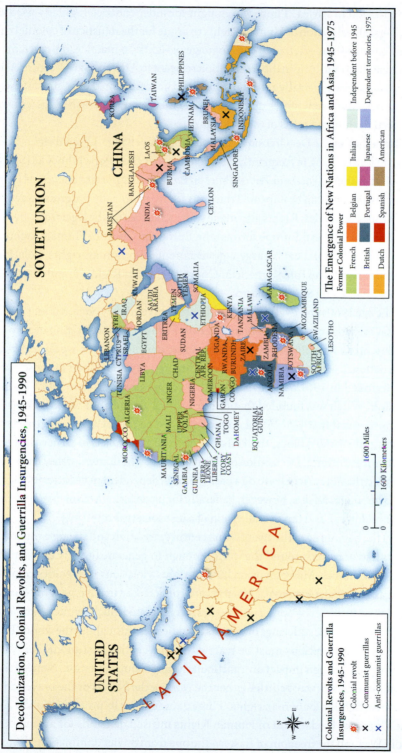

Map 6.2

Decolonization, Colonial Revolts, and Guerrilla Insurgencies, 1945-1990

The Emergence of New Nations in Africa and Asia, 1945–1975

Former Colonial Power

Italian	Independent before 1945	
Japanese	Dependent territories, 1975	
American		

French	Belgian	
British	Portugal	
Dutch	Spanish	

Colonial Revolts and Guerrilla Insurgencies, 1945-1990

- ✸ Colonial revolt
- ✗ Communist guerrillas
- ✗ Anti-communist guerrillas

were located in Africa. Those who fought for independence regularly used the Universal Declaration of Human Rights to argue for the injustice of colonial rule. New constitutions often used the language of rights. In practice, however, many new nations found little in the Declaration relevant to African, Caribbean, or Asian needs or desires, especially as the document did not condemn the racism of Western countries. Many new states quickly became dictatorships, crushed dissent, and ignored the human rights of their citizens.

Nonetheless, the Declaration remained a force for change. US civil-rights leader Martin Luther King Jr. frequently cited it in his speeches. Pope John XXIII recast the Declaration as *Pacem in Terris* (*Peace on Earth*), an important encyclical (papal letter) issued in 1963 that formed the basis for many socially progressive actions in Catholic countries. Rights also made some advances on the legal front. In 1959 countries in Western Europe formed the European Court of Human Rights, in which an individual can charge a government with human-rights violations. A similar court, the Inter-American Court of Human Rights, founded in 1979, serves Central and South America.

The late 1960s and 1970s saw a proliferation of voluntary organizations known as NGOs (nongovernmental organizations) that used the Declaration to advocate for downtrodden minorities in various locations around the world. Amnesty International, which advocates against incarceration of "prisoners of conscience," was founded in 1961 and honored with a Nobel Peace Prize in 1977. In 1978 Helsinki Watch was founded to monitor nations' compliance with the Helsinki Accords issued that year. A document intended to reduce tension between the Soviet and Western blocs, the Helsinki Accords resembled in structure and in practice the Universal Declaration of Human Rights. The drafters of the Declaration intended the thirty Articles to be a package, interdependent necessities for dignity and a good life. NGOs, however, generally focus on a single issue (such as child labor or dowry), and the overall vision of a just society is often lost.

By the beginning of the twenty-first century, agitation and struggle for human rights had occurred around the world, enough to generate literally thousands of academic studies. Many focus on human-rights violations in specific countries, such as Zanzibar, Guatemala, Nigeria, and India.[19] The involvement of NGOs in particular struggles by oppressed peoples has generated much "witness" literature, which presents the sufferings of victims to audiences throughout the world. These wrenching descriptions must be read with some caution, as funding for NGOs may depend on their impact on a particularly horrendous situation. None of these limitations in any way belittles either the work of the NGOs or the brave actions of others fighting for human rights. Three decades after its promulgation in 1948, the Universal Declaration of Human Rights infused demands for an end of the Cold War and the freedom of Eastern Europe from Soviet domination.[20]

The Bigger Picture

The Legacy of the Universal Declaration of Human Rights

Visionary documents of the past such as the French Declaration of the Rights of Man and of the Citizen, the US Constitution, and the Universal Declaration of Human Rights seem to have great solidity. They have definitive paragraphs, numbered sections, and many signatures by important people. These sorts of documents were and are, however, the result of demands, negotiations, and compromises. With only a small change in the relative power of one faction or another or a slightly varied mix of personalities, the document might have come out quite differently. How important these utopian documents actually become depends on subsequent political and economic events, so it should be expected that their importance ebbs and flows—critical in one decade and largely ignored in a later one. Still, these major documents create an aura, a set of mental expectations: how much government can control the lives of its citizens, the proper treatment of children, the proper treatment of workers by employers. That these expectations are in the minds of citizens is far more important than the physical presence of the document in some museum or government building. Collectively, they define a proper and meaningful life of the individual and the moral behavior of a nation.

The linking of various rights into a package called "human rights" has both potential and problems. The potential is for worldwide agreement on explicit moral expectations of governments, employers, and citizens. Problems arise from glossing over the fact that previous statements of rights came from specific historical situations. Earlier formulations of rights did not, as we have seen, lead to the formulation of human rights as set forth in the UN Declaration. Invocation of the past to gain legitimacy for the invention of something new is frequently couched as a recovery of a past custom or a past glory. So how may we gain clarity on what is from the past and what is new? This central question requires considerable critical research and reflection. What was the main issue addressed in the document of the past? Who was the document's intended audience? Why was that issue important at the time? Now comes the hard part. Is the current situation similar to the one that produced the earlier document, or—always a possibility—does someone involved in drafting the current resolution want us to accept that now is, indeed, like then? Is there anything that could or should be learned from the past situation or its documents? Note that this process of accessing the fit between past events and present situation is much the same as the looking to precedent for guidance in the merits of a court case. Judges must decide in what manner a current case resembles an earlier one.

It is probably best to acknowledge that none of the earlier political or philosophical literature on rights contains three crucial features of modern human rights. First, merely by existing as a human being, one obtains a whole list of rights. Second, only the Declaration contains the radical assertion that rights obtained by being human stand above and supersede all rights and responsibilities to a nation, state, or religion. What needs to be emphasized here is that earlier statements of rights were actually demands for better treatment within a nation-state structure. They did not envision success in terms of establishing an institutional structure that would, both morally and legally, hold states to account for treatment of their enemies and treatment of their own citizens. The third unique feature of the Universal Declaration is that rights accruing by being human supersede the rights claimed by self-identified cultural groups.

All societies have to make critical decisions about how to treat our fellow citizens, how to treat other countries, and how to envision a better future for all. Underlying these decisions are choices about whether raw power will dominate policy or if moral consensus will restrain actions. For example, should the United States have invaded Afghanistan, home to al Qaeda, in the wake of the September 11, 2001 attacks waged by the terrorist group? Do secret courts established in times of national crisis violate the right to open and fair trials? Power and profit do not always win. It is useful to recall that a worldwide boycott of South African companies and goods did much to end apartheid in South Africa in the early 1990s. The boycott of South Africa is only one of thousands of boycotts and actions based on morality in opposition to power. Some actions have targeted corporations for violations of the rights of workers;[21] others have focused on conditions in prisons or the impact of free trade on the domestic labor force.[22] Does culture trump human rights, or do human rights trump culture? Does the cultural norm of genital

TIMELINE

1929–1933
The Great Depression

1937–1945
World War II

April 28, 1945
Drafting of the United Nations charter in San Francisco

January 10, 1946
First meeting of the United Nations General Assembly

April 1, 1946
Human Rights Commission elects Eleanor Roosevelt as its chair

January 27–February 19, 1947
First full meeting of the UN Human Rights Commission

February 1, 1947
Lebanese diplomat Charles Malik lays out the "human rights as individual rights" position

June 1, 1947
Full drafting meeting of the UN Human Rights Commission

1948–1965
Height of European decolonization

mutilation supersede the right of women to refuse it in a nation-state? Does the culture of caning students in Singapore take precedence over the human right of students not to be subject to physical violence in school? Does the state get to decide a unified culture for all its citizens, thereby condemning minority cultures to extinction?[23] Does government planning, which is intended to benefit all citizens, trump the human rights of individuals? If a nation's leaders decide that more or less population is necessary, do they have the right to force women to conceive or not? Does a state have the right to prevent its citizens from dangerous or unhealthy behavior—such as smoking, not wearing a seat belt, or growing obese? Or is there a human right to undertake risky behavior?

Worldwide, there seems to be an unstoppable trend to couch political aspirations in the language of human rights and pressure to expand human rights to include, for example, resistance to the death penalty, LBGTQ rights, rights of natives to land, and the right to education, healthcare, and a living wage. This restless and effective activism is the real legacy of the Universal Declaration of Human Rights, a vision of human dignity alive with hopes, aspirations, and actions for a better world.[24]

For digital learning resources, please go to
www.oup.com/he/gordon-seventhemes1e

December 10, 1948
UN General Assembly passes the Universal Declaration of Human Rights

January 21, 1959
Countries in Western Europe form the European Court of Human Rights

July 1961
Amnesty International is founded

1966
United Nations establishes a structure to adjudicate human-rights violations

1977
Amnesty International is awarded Nobel Peace Prize

1978
Helsinki Watch is formed

1979
Central and South America form the Inter-American Court of Human Rights

1992
United States ratifies human-rights violations covenant

Empire and Environment

The Big Picture: Human Activity and the Environment

Even before the ecological impact of agriculture, human gathering and hunting activities affected the environment. A current-day gatherer-hunter tribe in the Amazon rainforest, for example, collects various fruits in a yearly cycle and brings them back to one or another of their camps. After they eat the fruits, they throw away the pits and seeds. Over millennia, the concentration of fruit trees around camps has become far higher than in the surrounding forest. Hunting had more severe and widespread environmental effects. Prehistoric humans hunted large animals to extinction in many parts of the world. In North America, humans killed off the wooly mammoth, giant beaver, cave bear, lion, and horse. The pattern was much the same in Europe. Across Asia, hunters decimated horses, which survived only in the remote mountains of Central Asia. In Australia, humans hunted to extinction marsupial lions, giant lizards, and several varieties of large, flightless birds.

The spread of agriculture produced even more profound environmental effects. Rivers in Egypt, India, the Middle East, the Americas, Africa, China and Europe were channeled and altered to trap fish and irrigate crops. Farmers weeded out local plants in favor of food crops. The process had its share of environmental disasters.

> **Tea-pickers fan across a hillside in British India, ca. 1900. The introduction of plantation-style agriculture by European empires transformed environments around the world.**

Clearing forests around coastal cities promoted an influx of seawater. Scholars believe that Carthage (rival and enemy of the Roman Empire) collapsed not because of defeat by Rome but because deforestation produced salination and rendered its agricultural land barren. Overpopulation of early capitals strained water resources; drought has been implicated in the decline of the Indus Valley civilization in South Asia as well as the end of the Inca, Maya, and Anasazi civilizations in the Americas.

This chapter focuses on the period after 1500 CE, when European powers began to conquer much of the world. By World War I (1914–1918) they controlled more than 80 percent of the land on the planet. They used their industrial, military, and political dominance to turn small multicrop farms into large monoculture commercial estates and plantations across the world, including rubber in Malaya and Burma (now Myanmar), cotton in Egypt, cocoa in West Africa, tea and timber in India and Ceylon (now Sri Lanka), coffee and tobacco in Brazil, sugar in the Caribbean, and coffee, to-bacco, and timber in Puerto Rico. The European powers also established large-scale mines where none had existed before, such as tin in Malaya, diamonds in Rhodesia (today part of Zimbabwe), and copper in southern Congo and Chile.

European dominance of much of the world raises many questions about imperial environmental effects. Did all colonies go through the same "phases"—exploration, conquest, exploitation? How about the period between conquest and independence? Were all imperial powers similar in their approach to "development"? How was "efficiency" defined in colonies, and how was this definition discussed in the European setting? How were new crops introduced into colonies? What was the role of technology in making a colony prosper or fail? What ecological changes remained after a colony's independence?

Our guide to the environmental impacts of the first phase of European exploration, conquest, and colonization is Tomé Pires, who was born around 1468, probably in Lisbon. Though not noble, his family had education and status. His father was apoth-ecary (pharmacist) to John II, king of Portugal, and the family probably owned a shop on a well-known street of apothecaries.[1]

Exploration and Conquest

In the Americas, in the early sixteenth century the Europeans sought gold and silver. Asia was more complicated. The Spanish and Portuguese needed to know what, how, where, and when goods and products might be bought and sold at a profit. They investigated crops, medicines, raw materials, metals, luxury products, and everyday goods. Some of Asia's products, such as tin, sulfur, and iron, were familiar. Other products Europeans had known only from descriptions in Arabic pharmacopeias or cookbooks. Many products were wholly new. (Access to these spices and other luxuries was, after all, why Columbus sailed west in 1492 in search of the successors of Qubilai Khan, China's famed thirteenth-century Mongol ruler.)

In the decades before Tomé Pires was born, the king of Portugal repeatedly sent ships down the west coast of Africa to search of the direct source of African gold.[2] Important results of these decades-long explorations were steady advances in ship design, navigation, sail technology, and gun casting. The Portuguese finally turned a profit on these ventures in the 1490s. In the same decade that Columbus, sailing for Spain, "discovered" what Europeans would call the "New World," the Portuguese explorer Vasco da Gama became the first European to reach the west coast of India by sea.

Back in Lisbon, Tomé Pires served as apothecary to Prince Afonso, heir to the throne, until the sixteen-year-old prince's untimely death in 1491. Exactly what Pires did after that, or why he left Portugal for India in April 1511, is unknown, but he had letters of introduction from two important people: the chief physician of the king and the head of the overseas department in Lisbon. Pires sailed with the fleet down the west coast of Africa, around the Cape of Good Hope, and into the Asian world.[3]

A few months after his arrival at the newly conquered port of Goa (on the west coast of India) Tomé Pires moved on to the even more recently conquered port of Malacca (in southeast Asia at the tip of the Malay Peninsula, near current-day Singapore). He wrote to his brother that he had obtained the position of "scribe and accountant of the trading warehouse and controller of the drugs." He described

A page from a Portuguese atlas, produced around 1519, showing many of the lands the Portuguese encountered in Asia during the time of Tomé Pires.

himself as in good health and rich, "more than you can imagine." During his time in Malacca Pires wrote a book titled *Suma Oriental* (*Summation of the Oriental World*), in which he recounted what he saw and heard of the kingdoms and products of mainland and island Southeast Asia, China, and Japan. This sort of information was critical to Portuguese attempts at profitable trade and control.[4]

The section of *Suma Oriental* on Sumatra, for example, describes the goods available in the port of Pase on the north coast of Sumatra:

> It has from eight to ten thousand bahars [approximately 1800 tons] of pepper every year. The pepper is not as good as that from Cochin [on the southwest coast of India]; it is larger, hollower and lasts less; it has not the same perfection of flavour and it is not so aromatic. It [the port] produces silk and benzoin [a fragrant gum resin used in medicines, perfume, and incense] and at Pase you will find all the merchandise there is in all the island, because it is collected here.[5]

Despite their conquest of two important hubs of Asian trade, Goa and Malacca, the Portuguese did not in any sense take over maritime Asia. The only impact of these traders on the Southeast Asian environment was to increase demand for high-value resins and medicinal plants. More demand led to monoculture on a few Southeast Asian islands, the only places where a highly desirable spice would grow.

The Tragic End of Tomé Pires

In 1515, the Commander of the Portuguese in Asia selected Pires to open trading relations with China. His small fleet arrived at the southern Chinese port of Guangzhou in 1517. The fleet departed, and Tomé spent a year unsuccessfully seeking permission to proceed north to the capital (current-day Beijing), often offending local officials with his arrogance and ignorance of local customs and rules. When the fleet reappeared in 1518, the captain, an ill-tempered and violent man, forced local port officials to issue the permissions for Pires and his small entourage to travel to the Chinese court. At court, he was scorned for the meager presents he brought. Things went downhill from there. A letter arrived from the king of Malacca, detailing how the Portuguese had seized his port and disrupted trade. Malacca was, at that time, a tributary state to China. Chinese judges declared that Tomé Pires and his entourage were not representatives of a legitimate king but instead sea pirates. They were imprisoned, placed in heavy fetters, and their goods seized. Chinese judges sent them back to Guangzhou for further punishment. Pires, his entourage, the sailors from the fleet, and all the Portuguese found in the port were rounded up, jailed, paraded through the streets, and executed. Their heads were displayed as a warning to other pirates.[6]

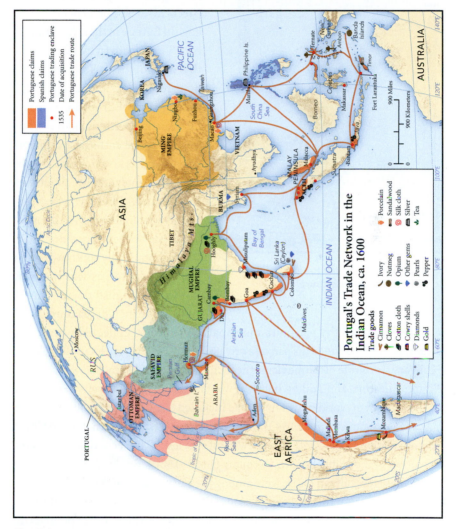

Portugal's Trade Network in the
Indian Ocean, ca. 1600

Map 7.1

Portrait of Tomé Pires, not long before his execution by the Chinese court.

Advances in Botany and Medicine

Tomé Pires and his book describing Asian plants and commodities was part of an explosion of plant knowledge in Europe in the sixteenth century. Three main factors account for this development. The first was a new restless, exploratory mood among some European doctors.[7] Dissatisfied with available treatments, several enthusiastic doctors began to travel in search of new herbs and treatments and write about what they found. These travels were mainly within Europe. At the opening of the sixteenth century Spain was as botanically unknown to an Austrian doctor, as was the New World. An English doctor named William Turner, for example, traveled with his wealthy patron to many parts of Europe, collected plants, and attempted cultivation in his patron's private garden.[8] A French doctor traveled to Hungary and wrote of the medicines he found. A few doctors reached what is today Egypt, Palestine, and Turkey, but none went farther east.[9] The wider exploration of the unknown world of distant plants included the Catholic Jesuit mission to the court of China (arrived 1543).[10] The letters, reports, and journals from China contain dozens of descriptions of new plant species.[11] The second factor was the invention of moveable type in Germany (1460–1500). Books about plants and medicines, generally in Latin, were among the earliest and most popular printed books. Accounts of medical explorations with their discovered treatments were almost immediately copied, often with woodcut illustrations. These pirated editions inserted accompanying charms or instructions lifted from various alchemy books. Overall, moveable type and pirated editions meant that descriptions of plants and new remedies circulated widely and quickly. Some of these books were translated into French, English, and other European languages not long after their original publication in Latin. Third, European rulers were directly interested in new plants that provided medicines, spices for food, scented oils for the body, and incense for churches. Rulers gained prestige from the unique plants in royal gardens.

Colonization and the Environment

Two centuries after Vasco da Gama discovered the sea route to Asia, Europeans still struggled to control reliable sources of Asian spices and medicines, cotton cloth, gemstones, and incense. Let us undertake a brief survey of the colonized world in say 1700. China remained independent, retaining the highly productive agricultural areas of its major river valleys. Japan had closed itself to foreigners. The Dutch had seized much of island Southeast Asia, where single-crop European-

An illustrated page from a medieval pharmacopoeia, a type of handbook that lists medicinal drugs with their formulations and uses.

owned plantations were well underway. The Mughal Empire dominated India, with European trading companies holding only a few enclaves on the coast. To the west of the Mughal Empire, Safavid Persia was a strong empire with no European incursions. To the west of the Safavid Empire was the Ottoman Empire, based in its capital of Istanbul. The Italian city-states of Venice and Genoa had defeated the Ottoman navy in the Mediterranean, and the Portuguese had defeated the Ottoman navy in the Indian Ocean. Still, the Ottomans had not lost land to or been colonized by the Europeans. To the north of the three big empires (Mughal, Safavid, Ottoman), the Rus tribe was just beginning its conquests of the vast grasslands to the east of Moscow. In this region Europeans were barely traders, much less colonizers. Europeans had not explored Africa. Across the Atlantic, in South and Central America, the Spanish and Portuguese had long-established private and Church-owned haciendas. These estates were largely self-sufficient in food but were based on major plantation crops of the New World—sugar, tobacco, coffee, cacao—and hides for leather.

If this picture of European contact with the rest of the world around 1700 seems uneven, it should. Some broad regions barely saw a European from one decade to the next. In others, Europeans were an expected part of the mix of traders in ports and cites. In still other areas, European conquest was well along with rulers overthrown and new European organizational patterns (haciendas, plantations, joint-stock companies) well on their way. In short, there was no single pattern of either early European colonization or the associated environmental damage. Researchers have attempted to establish universal "phases" through which all colonies passed. They posit an "exploitation frontier" that centered on grants of large blocks of land to Europeans or European-owned companies for maximum extraction of animal, mineral, and plant resources. (The reader may recall, for example, the large royal land grants of the eastern seaboard of the United States.) In this model of colonial invasion, the exploitation frontier moved inland as Europeans and their laborers hunted animals to extinction, mined easily reached mineral deposits, and exhausted the soil. This model explains some colonial environmental impacts fairly well, such as the hunting of the beaver to extinction in the Midwestern United States for tall fur hats in Europe. As we shall see, the theory also fits quite well the mining of tin in Malaya and Dutch Indonesia. The theory does not, however, explain haciendas, in which families did not pull up stakes to follow an exploitation frontier but rather stayed put for generations. It also does not account for wealthy Spanish in the Philippines who followed no exploitation frontier but instead lived in the main port cities and profitably invested in Chinese silks and porcelain bound for Mexico and on to Spain. The environmental impact of the Spanish in the Philippines was minimal.

What about the complexity of cotton cultivation in India in the nineteenth century, which also does not fit a simple exploitation frontier model? Our guide to the possibilities and problems of cotton is British botanist John Forbes Royale, who knew the subject intimately from his own cotton-growing experiments in the early decades of the nineteenth century.

John Forbes Royale, 1798–1858 CE.

Cotton Stresses in India

John Forbes Royale was born in 1798 at Kanpur, on the banks of the Ganges River in northern India. The British East India Company had conquered the wealthy Bengal region at the mouth of the Ganges in the 1750s.[12] Through various coerced treaties with the local ruler, they had seized districts up the Ganges River Valley. At the time of Royale's birth, Kanpur was a large town with a substantial British military presence. He was sent to Scotland to study medicine, but he also developed a keen interest in botany. After service as a doctor attached to British colonial armies, Royale was appointed in 1823 to head the botanical garden at Saharanpur (in today's Punjab state), which the British East India Company had established in 1750 with the aim of promoting the introduction of new crops of commercial value. He retired from the position in 1831, returned to England, and wrote several books on the productive products of India, one of which was titled *On the Culture and Commerce of Cotton in India* (1851).

The world Royale described differed radically from that of Tomé Pires two centuries earlier. Instead of Portugal's few sixteenth-century outposts and trading stations at Asian ports, the British East India Company of the eighteenth century conquered and ruled whole provinces across India. The Company had long identified cotton, indigenous to India, as the most important export crop of the subcontinent. In this opinion they were absolutely right. As the environmental historian Corry Ross puts it:

> By the middle of the nineteenth century cotton textile production was the largest manufacturing industry in the world, employing more people directly and indirectly, than any other ... In north-west England alone there were over 2,600 factories with around a half a million employees.[13]

Cotton had an overwhelming advantage over fabrics made of animal fiber. Think about raising sheep, shearing, cleaning the wool, and turning it into yarn: to produce an equivalent quantity of cloth from animal fiber required twelve times the energy of cotton.

US Domination of Cotton Exports

Around 1850 (the time of *Culture and Commerce of Cotton*) the southern United States dominated world cotton exports to Europe. Its slave plantations turned out over 200 million bales of raw cotton a year, five times the combined exports to Europe from India, Brazil, and the Caribbean islands combined.[14] This figure is, however, misleading. As Royale pointed out, Indian cotton exports to Europe were over and above clothing India's population of perhaps 120 million as well as providing that population with table and bed linens, quilts, curtains, tents, floor coverings, and horse trappings. India also exported large amounts of cotton goods to Africa and China.[15]

Still, the US domination of cotton exports to England troubled British administrators in India, the management of the East India Company in London, investors

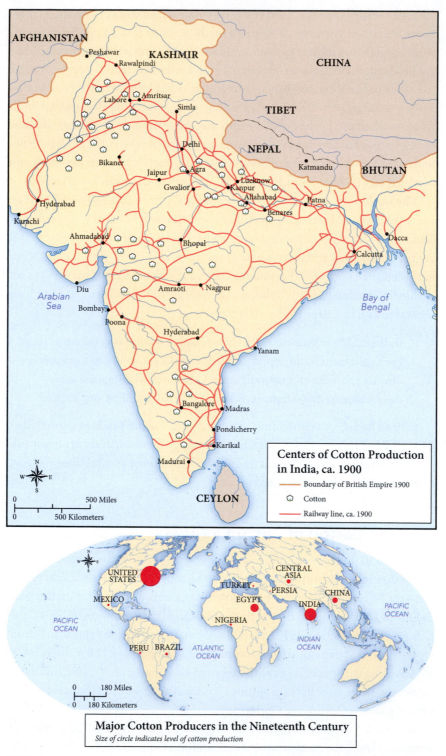

Centers of Cotton Production in India, ca. 1900

Boundary of British Empire 1900

⬡ Cotton

Railway line, ca. 1900

Major Cotton Producers in the Nineteenth Century

Size of circle indicates level of cotton production

Map 7.2

looking for new money-making opportunities in India, and amateur and professional botanists both in India and in England. They all knew that Indian farmers had grown cotton and weavers had loomed it for millennia. In the opinion of experts, Indian cotton had a number of problems. The most serious was deficient seed stock, which produced short, coarse fibers, inferior to southern US varieties with their longer fibers. A second problem was the slow, inefficient hand separation of the fibers from the cotton boll. A third problem was India's archaic hand looms, which could not complete with England's power looms, whose unstoppable advantages were, according to Royale, the "the joint influences of persevering ingenuity of her mechanics, and the untiring power of steam."[16]

"Improving" Indian Cotton

The board of the East India Company saw the cotton problem in relatively simple terms. The new agricultural stations and local planters needed to figure out how to grow US-grade cotton in India. Once the regimen was proven, peasant farmers should receive training and British entrepreneurs should provide capital to mechanize the ginning of cotton and generally improve yield, quality, and speed of processing. The directors saw these changes as good for all: cultivators, investors, government, traders, and weavers. The British commitment to the new strains of cotton and mechanization went beyond the economic benefits. Talk of Britain's moral duty to "improve" and "civilize" the colonies appeared often in the British newspapers of the nineteenth century and in official government reports.[17]

While cotton entrepreneurs in India coveted US cotton, they never considered using slaves to grow cotton, which raises the question of why not. Indian cotton was a crop of tens of thousands of small growers, and no place in India lent itself to large-scale cotton plantations. Also, strong public opposition to slavery was the order of the day in England. In addition, a well-established legal system in India precluded the wholesale rounding up of cotton growers (as white settlers rounded up natives in Kenya and forced them to work on their farms).

We must step back from the specific story of "improving" Indian cotton to consider underlying assumptions shared by all European colonizers. First, think about the deep, complex, and powerful effects of racism. Whether one focuses on the British in India, the French in Indochina, or the Dutch in Indonesia, colonizers shared the bedrock assumption that they were smarter, stronger, better administrators, more just, and morally superior to those they ruled. Their language produced superior literature and better legal decisions that would shake the "sloth," Royale predicted, from the peoples they ruled.

Second, the colonizers were inventors and importers of machines so demonstrably superior to local methods that European technology would rapidly transform the life and culture of the colonized. Third, Europeans, as individuals or joint stock companies, saw themselves as morally entitled to substantial guaranteed profits for developing and exporting nonreplaceable natural resources. It is important to note that this moral, linguistic, and technological template for exploitation also developed in places where revolution had dismantled colonies, such as all of South and Central America.

Only by understanding the interlocking moral, linguistic, and technological template of colonialism does "improving" Indian cotton make sense. The process was, however, far more difficult than the East India Company had envisioned. Many of the restraints were environmental. Cotton needed, and still needs, a great deal of water over its long growing cycle (2,500 gallons of water to produce one pound of cotton). The most successful US cotton plantations were laid out as long narrow strips of land with the short side adjoining the Mississippi River. These plantations tapped the Mississippi for irrigation throughout the cotton-growing cycle. An essential aspect of the slave labor of US plantations was the periodic clearing of the irrigation cannels and

Cartoon showing of the "burden" of England and the United States carrying backward, dark-skinned colonized people out of barbarism and into the modern age, 1900.

maintenance of the levees (embankments built to prevent the overflow of a river), since these plantations had previously been swampland and were well below the level of the Mississippi. It was impossible to recreate these conditions in India. Rainfall was confined to the monsoon months (June through September), when rivers were in flood. During the rest of the year, rivers dropped and irrigation was not possible. The political situation was also not promising. Even though the East India Company controlled some portions of the major rivers of north India, indigenous rulers and large landholders owned much of the rest, making coordinated irrigation and levee building impossible.

Indian Cotton Before the Colonizers

Over millennia, Indian farmers had adjusted to the ecological restraints of growing cotton. They had long ago figured out that certain types of soil would retain enough monsoon moisture for cotton to grow and produce bolls. These water-retaining soils had indigenous names, such as the "black soil" of the Malwa region in Central India. In regions of heavier monsoon but less water-retentive soil, farmers banded together under the leadership of a ruler and built dams to impound swollen monsoon rivers or dug wells to tap groundwater below the surface. These wells and artificial ponds provided irrigation to only a small portion of agricultural land, however. The rest of the farmers, without irrigated land, treated cotton as a risky cash crop and adopted two strategies. First, they selected for drought-resistant varieties of cotton. Second, they never planted only cotton but rather grew it at the edges of fields or interplanted it with food crops. If cotton succeeded, it provided a welcome source of cash. If it failed, at least the farmer and his family had food for the year. British "experts," quoted in *Culture and Commerce*, saw intermixed fields as careless, indifferent agriculture:

> In this division the cultivation of cotton is little more than nominal: it is most commonly mixt up with other crops; it is nowhere carefully tended; in many places it is the object of superstitious aversion.[18]

There is no evidence for this claim.

It is also important to understand how cotton was marketed before the British colonial period. Cotton dealers and money lenders in small towns traveled the countryside and advanced money to farmers to pay taxes, buy seed, cover the expenses of festivals, and marry sons and daughters. Farmers delivered cotton to a town not more than twenty miles away from their fields,

Cotton ginning in India, ca. 1840.

the farthest distance a farmer could go and return in an ox cart in a day. Each of these small towns produced a specific specialized cotton fabric. One town loomed only heavy, coarse cloth for tents or curtains. Another made fine cloth for headscarves, and yet another made only bed sheets. The variety of cotton that farmers grew was thus tuned to its environmental niche and to the product loomed in a nearby town. The finished products were sold to wholesale cloth dealers in cities and from there shipped to specific final destinations. One town in eastern Malwa, for example, wove only fine white cotton headscarves, which were carried to the port of Surat on the Indian Ocean. From there, these goods made their way to Poland, where women bought and wore the headscarves. Many of these specific cotton fabrics required a return flow of information as styles changed and desirable colors shifted. This information passed from big fabric dealers in cities to the relevant smaller fabric dealers in towns, who then shared it with weavers and dyers.

Given the subtle tuning of the variety of cotton to environmental conditions and a specific fabric, it is no surprise that hopeful experiments in India with US cotton simply failed. In Bengal, for example, the imported cotton plants produced a great deal of foliage but no bolls.[19] According to Royale:

> [The Agricultural Society of India] ascribe the failure to bad seed, to their positive ignorance respecting the proper season for sowing, to the land . . . being wholly unsuited to the growth of cotton, be *too rich* in some places and *too salt* in others. . . . [and] an improper mode of planting; the native broadcast plan [a method of seeding that involves scattering seed over a relatively large area, in contrast to precision seeding] being unsuited to the American cotton plants, which, besides requiring to be planted at a distance allow the exceedingly delicate tap-root to penetrate freely.[20]

A Turning Point: The US Civil War

Only a decade after publication of *Culture and Commerce of Cotton,* the US Civil War (1861–1865) not only impacted cotton on a worldwide scale, but also had profound local effects. The federal (Union) navy took New Orleans early in the war, cutting off cotton exports. Union ships successfully blockaded the

Confederacy's other ports. Southern cotton rotted on the wharves or was not even harvested. A substantial portion of the world's cotton suddenly disappeared from the market and created a boom in cotton in other parts of the world. In Egypt, for example, large landholders along the Nile converted their estates to cotton and nearly drained the river to irrigate the new cotton fields. In India, both British investors and local moneylenders sensed a great opportunity to expand cotton cultivation. Prices rose, and farmers went into debt to expand cultivation. They opened new fields farther from their village, requiring more labor. Could they locate and maintain the necessary labor? Would the soil retain enough moisture from monsoon rains for the cotton plants to set bolls? The new fields were planted only in cotton, and many of the existing fields, which had been both food crops and cotton, were converted to a monoculture of cotton. Could a monoculture survive pernicious insects? Farmers struggled to overcome numerous obstacles to successful cultivation.

The cotton boom in India and Egypt did not last long. As farmers added acreage, prices drifted downward, even during the US Civil War. The long-term environmental impact was to make agriculture more fragile across broad areas. If there was drought, the farmer suffered doubly. He had decreased acreage in drought-resistant food crops and also received no income from cotton. He still had debts from borrowing money to open new cotton fields. In western India, low monsoon rainfall turned whole districts into famine zones. Farmers lost their lands to moneylenders. In desperation farmers demanded help from the colonial government, which had neither the will nor the resources to provide effective assistance. No one questioned the basic shift from mixed fields to monoculture or the resilience of the older system of growing specialized cotton for local looming. Expansion of production and export of raw cotton was the order of the day. With full concurrence of British investors, "development" remained the central policy of the colonial government right up to India's independence from British rule in the mid-twentieth century.

Tin Mining and the Environment in Malaya

Let us now turn to the environmental effects of mines, another mode of "development" in European colonies, with a focus on tin. For millennia, tin had been an essential component of bronze, and without it none of the weapons, vessels, armor, or ritual objects of the Bronze Age would exist. Such objects are material proof of an enduring trade in tin that began at least as early as 3000 BCE. Across the world, tin has always been relatively rare. One region of tin was an east–west belt across northern Europe, which included smaller deposits in

Spain, Portugal, and France, somewhat larger deposits in Germany, and the largest European deposits in Cornwall, England. A second tin belt ran south from China, down the Malay Peninsula and into the islands of Sumatra and Java (current-day Indonesia). The Chinese tin deposits were discovered only in modern times, but Malayan tin was justly famous across the ancient world. Perhaps the earliest written reference to Malayan tin is by the Arab geographer Abu Dalaf, who wrote in 940 CE, "In the entire world there does not exist a tin mine as this one in Kalah [Malaya]."[21]

Ancient Tin Mining

Our silent guide to tin in Malaya is an exciting shipwreck. Off the coast of Java an indigenous sailing ship went down around 1000 CE. The wreck lay undisturbed on the flat ocean floor for almost a thousand years. Then, noticing that birds dove frequently over a small area, local fishermen assumed that the fish were probably congregating in a wreck below. The race was on between government archaeologists and looters. The archaeologists, in this case, won. Over the course of three diving seasons the wreck yielded thousands of objects of porcelain, bronze, and tin. In what remained of the hold were thousands of tin ingots, all of the same weight. Divers also found two types of mirrors on the seafloor. One, of lower quality with an indistinct image, was characteristically Indonesian in design. The second, with a much clearer image, was of Chinese origin. The Chinese mirrors were 25 percent tin, alloyed with copper and lead. This mixture yielded a brittle metal that took a lustrous, reflective polish and yielded a superior image. It is likely that Malayan tin was shipped to China in ingot form, melted into this special alloy, and cast into high-value items such as mirrors, some of which were then exported back to Southeast Asia.[22]

The ancient method of Asian tin mining was labor-intensive. A miner stood in the river, placed river water and sediment in a shallow pan, and gently rocked it. Tin, being heavier than the surrounding clay, settled to the bottom of the pan. The water and clay were poured off, leaving flakes of tin on the bottom of the pan. These flakes were gathered, melted, and cast into ingots of a near-standard weight. This mining process was inefficient but had no significant environmental impacts.

The Rush for Tin

All of this changed in the nineteenth century. The tin mines of Europe, especially Cornwall, played out just as demand for tin dramatically increased. Tin was an important component of cast cannon and also the new motors and pumps of the Age of Steam. It was, however, the humble tin can that generated enormous new demand for tin. Coating a steel can with tin preserved the food inside for months, rapidly changing how food was supplied to armies, navies, transoceanic travel, and cities. This rapidly increasing demand for tin created what has been termed a "tin frontier."[23] Both European and Chinese entrepreneurs installed simple technology to recover tin more quickly than traditional panning allowed. They hired workers to divert a stream into a narrow water channel close to a site of tin-bearing ore. Laborers dug the ore and dumped it into the water channel. Inside the channel were a series of small dams, which slowed down the diverted water and the heavy tin particles and nodules collected behind the dams. It took much labor to clean the tin and eventually cast it into ingots. Still, the system was much more efficient than simple panning.

Let us step back from the specifics of early tin mining in Malaya to a broader analysis. First, Malayan tin, like Indian cotton, had an international market long before the arrival of Europeans. Second, indigenous Malayan tin panners resisted shifting to new, more capital-intensive methods, just as Indian cotton growers opposed growing cotton as their sole crop. Third, tin entrepreneurs broke this resistance by bringing in Chinese labor, just as southern US cotton entrepreneurs brought in African slaves for their plantations.

How was the environment damaged from the new, more invasive mining techniques of the European and Chinese tin entrepreneurs? Cutting side channels tore open the vegetation. The workers cut down some trees for construction of crude sleeping cabins, more for cooking and heating water for tea, and even more as fuel for the smelting furnace. The mounds of "tailing" (river sand and clay after removal of the tin) also damaged the environment, as no native plants would grow on the mounds. There were, however, technological limits to the environmental impact. Miners could cut only a few yards deep into a tin-rich hillside before the sides of the excavation collapsed. Also, the mine had to be close enough to the sluice channels to economically transport the tin ore. This mining method encouraged swift recovery of easily accessible tin, then shutting the operation and moving on. After speculators abandoned a site, trees soon clogged the channels, leaving a patchworked landscape of barren tailings and recovering forest.[24]

In the mid-nineteenth century several new tin-mining technologies arrived in Malaya. The first was an old Chinese invention named the *chinchia,* which consisted of a bucket-and-chain rig driven by a water wheel in a stream. The *chinchia* allowed water removal down to about forty feet, thereby holding back flooding and allowing mining of deeper deposits of tin ore. Once the ore was carried to the surface, the cleaning and smelting resembled the earlier

Chinese-style tin mining, late nineteenth century.

channel method. Thousands of Chinese men migrated to Malaya to mine tin using the *chinchia*. Their solitary encampments were the main human feature of Malaya's forests.

European Intervention Escalates

Mid-nineteenth century European investors could not and would not accept that the millennia-old Chinese *chinchia* was the most effective way to mine tin, however. European companies demanded and received the grant of large tracts of tin-bearing ore, long leases, and guarantees of no government interference. These European investors then imported proven European mining machinery to make the whole industry "efficient." Each of these ventures—with their engineers and survey teams—was a spectacular failure. The sophisticated machinery made extraction of tin far more expensive than the Chinese water-wheel method. The only environmental damage was some shafts and a large amount of equipment left behind.[25] Recall how the European racism of the day (which discounted any useful Chinese knowledge) reinforced the sureness that European machinery would certainly be efficient and profitable. The moral obligation to "develop" the land led to granting British companies long leases, no competition, and no

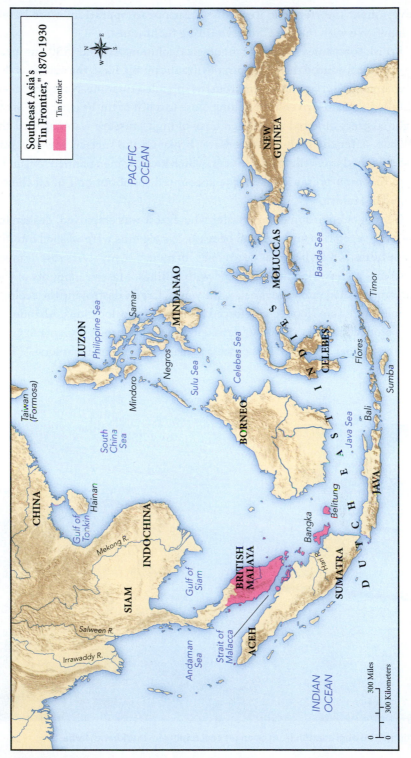

Southeast Asia's "Tin Frontier," 1870–1930

Tin frontier

Map 7.3

government interference. Regardless, European operations were barely competitive with the old Chinese mining techniques.

British companies sought a technological solution. Around 1880 European investors introduced the high-power hydraulic pump. First, the company dug a catchment reservoir upstream from the intended tin mine. Next, engineers installed a steam-driven water pump close to a hill of tin-bearing ore. Six to eight laborers directed a two-inch hose of high-pressure water against the hillside. After the high-pressure water broke up the surface, low-pressure water washed everything into sluices, which local women panned for tin. By 1916 this high-pressure technique accounted for about half of all the tin mined in Malaya.

It brought environmental disaster wherever it was employed, destroying both the vegetation and the land beneath. Whole hills were washed into the sluice boxes. Rivers became "dead zones" of mud.[26] Many rivers rose as much as several meters, flooding farmland with tailings. Massive amounts of clay and sand washed into valleys below the works, largely destroying the ecology. Whole cities were flooded and forced to move to new locations. Abandoned sites eroded for years and never developed enough topsoil for plants to grow. One researcher has called this process a "mass destruction technique." (This

Environmental degradation from open pit coal mining in Jharkhand, India.

mining technique was developed for gold mining in California but was banned in the 1880s as too destructive.)

The final chapter of this story of environmental degradation also centers on a new technology that came from Europe. Malaya's remaining tin was located in lowland valleys and swamps, where it concentrated after dropping from streams as they slowed down. British companies attacked these difficult landscapes with huge dredges, each the size of a small office building, which were originally developed for sucking up muck to deepen harbors and rivers. These dredges raised and processed enormous amounts of muck, leaving a sterile swamp or river delta. The colonial government, in a largely useless measure of amelioration, used the same dredges to channelize rivers, thereby further destroying the ecologies of riverbanks and watersheds.

By the 1930s—in one hopeful sign in this dismal picture—the colonial government of Malaya started to move away from "development" thinking to "stewardship" thinking. It began active oversight of tin mines, generating environmental regulations that limited the height of hills to be mined for tin and outlawed the dumping of tailings into rivers. None of these regulations prevented the dredge-mining destruction of swamps and lowlands or extension of dredging to shallow offshore sites, which were reduced to sterile sea zones. The only powerful force restraining the mining companies was the rubber lobby, whose vast rubber estates were threatened by high-pressure mining and dredging. The political jockeying between mine owners and rubber barons continued even after Malaya gained its independence in 1957.

The Bigger Picture

The Environmental Legacy of Colonialism

The environmental damage of extractive mining continues today. The effects of "topping" coal-bearing hills in the Appalachian Mountains (especially West Virginia and Tennessee) resemble those of hydraulic mining for tin in Malaya. The stripping of whole mountaintops and slopes to expose the coal seams creates massive amounts of waste, known as "overburden," which is supposed to be "retained" in large artificial ponds. All too often the ponds leak or fail and flood the valleys, destroying homes and towns and creating dead zones where no plants will grow. This pattern repeats across our world, whether the extracted material is gold, silver, copper, iron, or aluminum. If anything, capital flowing into mines is on the increase. China is actively developing infrastructure in Africa and Southeast Asia expressly intended to provide access to untapped minerals. In 2019 US President Donald Trump floated the idea of buying Greenland for its vast mineral deposits.

Monoculture also dominates our world. Mile upon mile of corn and soybeans have replaced native plants. The present and future of farmers from Chile to Australia to the Midwestern United States are fully tied to the worldwide prices of off-season fruit, or beef, or corn syrup for sugary drinks. Let us consider some essential features of the system of mining and monoculture.

Costs and Benefits

Growing wheat, cutting trees, fishing the oceans—all the processes that produce commodities threaten the environment. The crucial question is who gets the benefit and who pays the cost. As water transport became less and less expensive in the twentieth century (think oil tankers and container ships), it became easier and easier to import raw materials from far away—and thus to separate the benefits from the costs. We open a can (though today the can is aluminum, not tin) without thinking of our benefits, which are readily available, inexpensive, mass-market food. Nor do we consider the costs to a once beautiful ecology like Malaya—now, in many places, reduced to barren deserts of tailings. In extractive industries, low-wage laborers bear much of the cost, forced to live with minimum rights, no collective bargaining, and long-term mine-related disease. The miners bear these costs but receive none of the benefits.

Scientific Attitude

A shared ethos among European colonial governments made it a duty, even a moral obligation, of Europeans to bring "backward" colonies into the modern world, to "civilize" them. Modernization meant, in part, the use of machines powered by fossil fuels to minimize labor. These processes depended on the science of the day, including surveying, mapping, geology, statistics, chemistry, hydrology, and plant research. Particularly important is European colonial use of the term "efficiency," which in government reports, scientific papers, and internal business documents meant extracting all of a useful substance (tin, gold, cotton, rubber) from the land, not leaving a single bit behind. Efficiency was contrasted to indigenous methods, which were termed "lazy" or "sloppy" and did not put maximum extraction above all else. This pervasive "scientific" attitude discounted any preexisting indigenous knowledge of how to grow and fertilize crops, decrease risk in farming, and exploit networks to mitigate the effects of natural disaster. When the land suffered drought, monoculture for highest yields meant serious famine across cotton-growing areas of India. The famines of the late nineteenth century in India were in large part the result of colonial pressure to mono-crop cotton without backup irrigation.

The Role of Technology

Technology played a complex role in colonial impacts on the environment. In the first half of the nineteenth century cotton, for example, moved by sailing ship from India to England, a slow process prone to damage from sea water. Steamships of the second half of the nineteenth century dramatically lowered the cost of trans-porting cotton, the time in transit, and the likelihood of damage. On land, however, mechanization did not offer any particular advantages for the growing of cotton. Oxen-driven ploughs worked efficiently on the small plots, and the British colonial government was unable to seize land (as they did in Africa) and consolidate small holdings into large farms. India already had a sizable population, complex social organization, and lawyers who quickly understood how to protect land in courts from claims by Europeans.

In the mines of Malaya technology generally facilitated the mining of poorer and poorer tin ore. The result was that more and more of the land had to be destroyed to produce the same amount of tin.

No New Industries

Colonial exploitation of the environment did not result in new industries in colonies. Everything extracted in colonies was processed in the home country. Malayan planta-

Fridays for Future environmental protest, Berlin, 2019.

tions, for example, produced vast amounts of natural rubber, but none of it was processed in Malaya into tires or rubber electrical insulators. India grew massive amounts of cotton, but in the colonial period most of it was shipped to England as raw cotton, where it was loomed into cloth. The coffee of Brazil was treated as a generic commodity. Packaging and branding took place in Europe and America.

The focus on the environmental destruction during the colonial era suggests an elemental question. Is it the nature of capitalism to seek the quick profit and ignore the broader environmental and social damage? Were the colonies merely places with little regulation and a welcoming attitude toward capital investment and entrepreneurship?

Human-caused climate change is here—and now. A first step is to give up the idea that natural resources are endless and to be exploited to the full. A second step is to

TIMELINE

ca. 3000 BCE
Earliest evidence of trade in tin

ca. 940 CE
Earliest written reference to Malayan tin by Arab geographer Abu Dalaf

ca. 1000 CE
Sailing ship containing thousands of objects of porcelain, bronze, and tin sinks off coast of Java

1460–1500
Printed books begin to appear in Europe

1468
Tomé Pires is born

ca. 1490
The Portuguese begin turning a profit on trading ventures along the West Coast of Africa

1499
Portuguese explorer Vasco da Gama becomes the first European to reach the west coast of India by sea

April 1511
Tomé Pires leaves Portugal for India

1515
Pires is selected by the Portuguese to open trading relations with China

1517
Pires and his fleet arrive in Guangzhou, China

ca. 1518
Pires and his entourage are accused of being sea pirates by the Chinese, leading to their imprisonment and eventual execution

1543
Catholic Jesuit mission arrives in the court of China

question the viability of a "development" model in a world of limited resources. A third step is to respect local knowledge and methods. These changes are difficult, but crucial. The extent to which we make them directly affects the sustainability and future of our world.

For digital learning resources, please go to
www.oup.com/he/gordon-seventhemes1e

1750s
The British East India Company conquers the wealthy Bengal region in eastern India

1798
John Forbes Royale is born in Kanpur, India

1823
Royale is appointed head of the botanical garden at Saharanpur in Punjab, India

1831
Royale returns to England and goes on to write several books on the productive products of India

ca. 1850
New tin-mining technologies come to Malaya

1851
Royale publishes *On the Culture and Commerce of Cotton in India*

ca. 1855
The southern United States dominates world cotton exports to Europe

1861–1865
US Civil War

ca. 1880
European investors introduce the high-power hydraulic pump technology in Malaya

1914–1918
World War I

1916
High-pressure pumping techniques account for about half of all the tin mined in Malaya

ca. 1930
Government of Malaya moves toward active oversight of tin mines

Afterword

It has been quite a journey across the world since 1500 CE. We explored the crucial difference between sex and gender and the role of patriarchy in societies and cultures. We encountered societies that demanded heterosexuality, but also societies that incorporated homosexual love and sexuality. We found that gender fluidity featured prominently in Tokugawa Japan and also Renaissance Florence.

Ideas of nationalism and internationalism were also important to consider. We traced the struggles to define loyalty and settle which loyalty would supersede others. Commitment to family, religion, and ethnic heritage continue to jostle with commitment to a nation. Loyalty to the nation competes with the idea of one world implicit in the concept of universal human rights. These discussions and expectations appear regularly in the news of the day, from actions by nations of the former Soviet Union defending their freedom to new states declaring themselves Muslim.

The effects of colonialism appear again and again in the formulation of various nationalisms, the lingering legacy of Western racism, and the heritage of extractive, ecologically devastating industries. Colonialism denigrated local knowledge, which we must learn to respect, just as we must understand struggles with the economic fallout of forced labor and extractive industries.

We found that the search for new technology was a worldwide phenomenon not confined to the West. The theory and practice of optics passed from Muslim scientists to undergird the European Renaissance. Innovation was never solely local. It took place in a larger culture of people, who adopted things they needed and even things that they did not know they wanted. The individual inventor was sometimes critical, but often more important were the many incremental steps in the process.

We also confronted ideas of slavery and freedom. Sometimes legal freedom made only small but welcome differences in the daily lives of former slaves. The enslaving of native peoples was a feature of every colonial empire, from forcing indigenous peoples into reservations in Kenya and the United States to making them work on plantations in the Congo and Java. Protections from slavery figure prominently in the *Universal Declaration of Human Rights*.

As we have seen, choices and problems of the past do not stay in the past. They affect our present, just as choices we make today will shape our future. Making wise choices demands that we look beyond headlines to read, question, dig for information, and face the hard questions. At the deepest level, we have explored seven themes that resonate through time and across the world, regardless of religion, ethnicity, race, language, or region. It is at this level that we discover not only our differences, but also our shared experience and humanity.

Notes

Chapter 1

1. Judith Butler, *Gender Trouble: Feminism and the Subversion of Identity* (New York: Routledge, 1990).

2. For the variety of female-female love and sexuality, see *Lesbian Lives: Biographies of Women from the Ladder*, ed. Ruth Grier and Coletta Reid (Oakland, CA: Diana Press, 1976).

3. See the introduction to Ihara Saikaku, *Tales of Samurai Honor*, trans. Caryl Ann Callahan (Tokyo: Monumenta Nipponica, University of Tokyo, 1981). More detail is found in the introduction to Ihara Saikaku, *The Life of an Amorous Woman and Other Writings*, trans. Ivan Morris (New York: New Directions, 1963). See also Gary F. Leuff, *Male Colors: The Construction of Homosexuality in Tokugawa Japan* (Berkeley: University of California Press, 1995).

4. Considerable tension remained between the increasingly ostentatious lifestyle of the newly rich townsmen and the status and honor due to samurai. The shogunate initiated several strategies to reconcile wealth and honor in the rising cities; none of them were notably successful.

5. In the middle decades of his life Saikaku incorporated explicit sexual imagery into his linked stories. He has been accused of sensationalism, even pornography. Little of this work has been reprinted in Japan, and none of it translated.

6. Ihara Saikaku, *The Great Mirror of Male Love*, trans. Paul Gordon Schalow (Stanford, CA: Stanford University Press, 1990), 90–91.

7. Saikaku, *The Great Mirror of Male Love*, 61–62.

8. Homosexuality was also quite common in Buddhist monasteries in Japan at the time of Saikaku. The liaison was typically between an older teacher and a young acolyte. Single-sex institutions (such as the Catholic Church) would, of course, be prone to same-sex relations. See, for example, Regina Kinzel, *Criminal Intimacy: Prison and the Uneven History of Modern American Sexuality* (Chicago: University of Chicago Press, 2008).

9. Ihara Saikaku, *Gay Tales of the Samurai*, trans E. Powys Mathers (San Francisco: Alamo Square Press, 1995), 15–20. Several of Saikaku's prose works have been translated. See Nippon Eitaigura, *The Way to Wealth*, trans. Soji Mizumao (Tokyo: The Hokuseido Press, 1975); *This Scheming World*, trans. Masanori Takatsuka and David C. Stubbs (Rutland, VT: Charles E. Tuttle Co., 1965); *Five Men Who Loved Women*, trans. W. M. De Bary (Rutland, VT: Charles E. Tuttle Co., 1956); *The Life of an Amorous Woman*, trans. Kenji Hamada (Rutland, VT: Charles E. Tuttle Co., 2001); and *The Great Mirror of Male Love*, trans. Paul

Gordon Schalow (Stanford, CA: Stanford University Press, 1990).

10. Zahiu'd-din Muhammad Babur Padshah Ghazi, *Babur-Nama*, trans. Annette S. Beveridge (Delhi: Low Price Publications, reprinted edition, 1991), 120.

11. Babur-Nama, 121. For a broader view, see Syed Mubin Zehra, *Sexual and Gender Representations in Mughal India* (New Delhi: Manak Publications Pvt. Ltd., 2010).

12. Michael Goodich, *The Unmentionable Vice: Homosexuality in the Later Medieval Period* (New York: Dorset Press, 1979) has a good summary of the medieval Church's legal restraints on homosexuality. More important is Goodich's discussion of the Church's connection of sodomy with heresy and political opposition, especially in reference to France and several Italian cities. See his introductory chapter. Perhaps more than one might want to know of the strictures and punishments that the medieval Church promulgated is found in Glenn W. Olson, *Of Sodomites, Effeminates, Hermaphrodites, and Androgynes: Sodomy in the Age of Peter Damian* (Toronto: Pontifical Institute of Mediaeval Studies, 2011).

13. Epistle of the Apostle Paul to the Romans, 1, stanza 25–27.

14. Michael Rocke, *Forbidden Friendships: Homosexuality and Male Friendships in Renaissance Florence* (Oxford: Oxford University Press, 1996), 23–24. Rocke suggests that sodomy was one factor in the factional conflicts of Renaissance Florence in the fifteenth century.

15. For a wider view, both in space and time, see *The Pursuit of Sodomy: Male Homosexuality in Renaissance and Enlightenment Europe*, ed. Kent Gerard and Gert Hekma (New York: The Haworth Press, 1989).

16. Franciso Coreal, *Voyages de François Coreal aux Indiex Occidentales . . .* vol. 1 (Amsterdam: J. Frederic Bernard, 1772), 33–34. Translated in Will Roscoe, "How to Become a Berdache: Toward a Unified Analysis of Gender Diversity," in *Third Sex, Third Gender: Beyond Sexual Dimorphism in Culture and Society*, ed.

Gilbert Herdt (New York: Zone Books, 1994), 329. This book sets the high-water mark for a worldwide concept of a third gender.

17. Richard C. Trexler, "Making the American Berdache: Choice or Constraint?" *Journal of Social History* 35, no. 3 (Spring 2002): 613–636.

18. An apologia for Church condemnation of male-male sex and love is John Boswell, *Same-Sex Unions in Premodern Europe* (New York: Villard Books, 1994). For a critique of this position, see Mathew Kuefler, *The Boswell Thesis: Essays on Christianity, Social Tolerance, and Homosexuality* (Chicago: University of Chicago Press, 2006).

19. Gary Leupp, *Male Colors: The Construction of Homosexuality in Tokugawa Japan* (Berkeley: University of California Press), 189.

20. See *Same Sex Love and Desire among Women in the Middle Ages*, ed. Francesca Canadé Sautman and Pamela Sheingorn (London: Palgrave Macmillan, 2001).

21. This pillar-to-post life is well portrayed in the only memoir of the period by a woman, who was a sister of Babur. See Annette S. Beveridge, ed. and trans., *The History of Humāyūn* (Delhi: Idarah-i Adabiyāt-I Delhi, reprint edition, 1972).

22. Ruby Lal, *Domesticity and Power in the Early Mughal World* (Cambridge: Cambridge University Press, 2005), 27–28. See also Mart E. Giles, ed., *Women in the Inquisition: Spain and the New World* (Baltimore: Johns Hopkins University Press, 1999).

23. Akbar, third ruler of the Mughal dynasty, was the first to build a separate precinct for women, located in the sprawling new palace of Fatehpur Sikri. He married many women, mainly for the strategic purpose of consolidating the empire. Lal, *Domesticity and Power*, 169–179.

24. Translated in Carla Petievich, "Doganas and Zanakhis: The Invention and Subsequent Erasure of Urdu Poetry's 'Lesbian' Voice," in *Queering India*, ed. Ruth Vanita (New York and London: Routledge, 2002), 50.

25. For the relatively recent study of same-sex relations in India, see Vanita, ed., *Queering India*. See also Ana Garcia-Arroyo, *Alternative Sexualities in India: The Construction of Queer Culture* (Kolkata: Books Way, 2010); Momin Rahman, *Homosexuality, Muslim Cultures and Modernity* (London: Palgrave Macmillan, 2014).

26. Garcia-Arroyo, *Alternative Sexualities in India*, 45.

27. Church records of the time describe "riotous" relations between Franciscan friars and nuns at one of Pescia's convents, even the smuggling of a dildo into the convent. Judith C. Brown, *Immodest Acts: The Life of a Lesbian Nun in Renaissance Italy* (New York: Oxford University Press, 1986), 37–38.

28. Brown, *Immodest Acts*, 117–118.

29. For an excellent global treatment of the concept of third gender, see *Third Sex, Third Gender*, ed. Gilbert Herdt (New York: Zone Books, 1994).

30. Ma-Nee Chacaby with Mat Louisa Plummer, *A Two-Spirit Journey: The Autobiography of a Lesbian Ojibway-Cree Elder* (Winnipeg: University of Manitoba Press, 2016), 11.

31. Chacaby, *A Two-Spirit Journey*.

32. Chacaby, *A Two-Spirit Journey*, 65.

33. Chacaby, *A Two-Spirit Journey*, 60.

34. Chacaby, *A Two-Spirit Journey*, 25.

35. To revisit the two-spirit thesis, see Sabine Lang, *Men as Women and Women as Men: Changing Gender in Native American Cultures* (Austin: University of Texas Press, 1998). See also *Two-Spirit People: Native American Gender Identity, Sexuality, and Spirituality*, ed. Sue-Ellen Jacobs, Wesley Thomas, and Sabine Lang (Urbana: University of Illinois Press, 1997); Brian Joaseph Gilley, *Becoming Two-Spirit: Gay Identity and Social Acceptance in Indian Country* (Lincoln: University of Nebraska Press, 2006).

36. It is, of course, against the background of colonialism that former colonial governments struggle with current-day policy toward nonconforming genders. For example, see the two following studies from Africa: *Homosexuality: Perspectives from Uganda*, ed. Sylvia Tamale (Kamala: Sexual Minorities Uganda, 2007) and Marc Epprecht, *Hungochani: The History of a Dissident Sexuality in Southern Africa* (Montreal: McGill-Queen's University Press, 2nd ed., 2013).

37. Leila J. Rupp, *Sapphistries: A global History of Love between Women* (Vancouver: UBC Press, 2009, 97–104).

38. See Marcia M. Gallo, *Different Daughters: A History of the Daughters of Bilitis and the Rise of the Lesbian Rights Movement* (New York: Carroll & Graf Publishers, 2006); also Leila J. Rupp, *A Desired Past: A Short History of Same-Sex Love in America* (Chicago: University of Chicago Press, 1999).

Chapter 2

1. See Amiílcar Antonio Barreto, *Nationalism and Its Logical Foundations* (London: Palgrave Macmillan, 2009), 1-15.

2. On the mental side, see Gabriella Elgenus, *Symbols of Nations and Nationalism: Creating Nationhood* (London: Palgrave Macmillan, 2011). On the physical side, see Azar Gat, *Nations: The Long History and Deep Roots of Political Ethnicity and Nationalism* (Cambridge: Cambridge University Press, 2013). See also *Siniša Malešević, Nation-States and Nationalisms: Organization, Ideology and Solidarity* (Cambridge: Polity Press, 2013).

3. Craig Calhoun, *Nationalism* (Minneapolis: University of Minnesota Press, 1997), 4–5.

4. The degree to which nations are based on ethnic consciousness is hotly debated in

the literature on nationalism. There is also no consensus definition of ethnicity or ethnic consciousness. Proponents of preexisting ethnicity include Anthony D. Smith, *The Cultural Foundations of Nations: Hierarchy, Covenant, and Republic* (Oxford, Blackwell, 2008) and Anthony D. Smith, *Ethno-Symbolism and Nationalism: A Cultural Approach* (London: Routledge, 2009). See also Aviel Roshwald, *The Endurance of Nationalism* (Cambridge: Cambridge University Press, 2006).

5. Phen Cheah, *Spectral Nationality: Passages of Freedom from Kant to Postcolonial Literatures of Liberation* (New York: Columbia University Press, 2003).

6. The idea of legitimacy "rising" from the people is found in ancient Greece and Rome, but its rediscovery by eighteenth-century thinkers provoked a vigorous discussion of the topic. Earlier, in the mid-seventeenth century, English philosopher Thomas Hobbes explored the idea that a king's rights came not from God but from just representation of the whole of a people.

7. This vision of the right and responsibility of a people or a nation to reject unjust rule pervades, for example, the US Declaration of Independence.

8. Calhoun, *Nationalism*, 10.

9. Jeremy Murray-Brown, *Kenyatta* (London: George Allen & Unwin Ltd. 1972) 17–20. For the details and broad trends of Jomo Kenyatta's life I have relied on this excellent and carefully researched biography, which remains the best study of Kenyatta up to the period of Kenya's independence.

10. For the complex interconnections among the Kamba people, colonialism, and masculinity, see Myles Osborne, *Ethnicity and Empire in Kenya: Loyalty and Martial Race Among the Kamba c. 1800 to the Present* (Cambridge: Cambridge University Press, 2014).

11. Murray-Brown, *Kenyatta*, 105.

12. Jomo Kenyatta, *Facing Mount Kenya: The Traditional Life of the Gĩkũyũ* (Nairobi: Kenway Publications, second edition, 1978).

13. Kenyatta, *Facing Mount Kenya*, 78.

14. Dana A. Seidenberg, *Uhuru and the Kenya Indians; the role of a minority community in Kenya politics, 1939–1963* (New Delhi: Vikas, 1983).

15. Guy Arnold, *Kenyatta and the Politics of Kenya* (London: J. M. Dent & Sons Ltd., 1974), 96–97.

16. [no author], *Civil Society and Governance in Kenya Since 2002: Between Transition and Crisis* (Nairobi: African Research and Resources Forum, 2010).

17. Annie E. Coombes, Lotte Hughes, and Karega-Munene, *Managing Heritage, Making Peace: History, Identity and Memory in Contemporary Kenya* (London: I. B. Tauris, 2014). See also Samuel Alfayo Nyanchoga, *Citizenship, Ethnicity and Politics of Belonging in Kenya* (Nairobi: CUEA Press, 2014); Christian Thibon, Marie-Aude Fouére, Mildred Ndeda, Susan Mwangi, *Kenya's Past as Prologue: Voters, Violence and the 2013 General Election* (Nairobi: Twaweza Communications, 2014).

18. See, for example, Bethwell A. Ogot, *Kenyans, Who are We: Reflections on the Meaning of National Identity and Nationalism* (Kisumu, Kenya: Anyange Press, Ltd, 2012); see also Wambul Wamae and Xavier Verhoest, eds., *Who I Am, Who We Are* (Nairobi: Kuona Trust, 2016).

19. Benedict Anderson, *Imagined Communities: Reflections on the Origins and Spread of Nationalism* (London: Verso, rev. ed., 1991).

20. Anderson, Imagined, 26.

21. Umut Ōzkaririmli, *Contemporary Debates on Nationalism: A Critical Engagement* (London: Palgrave Macmillan, 2005), 84.

22. See Barreto, *Nationalism*, 15-22.

23. Difficult to reconcile with "one Nation, under God" is the US Civil War. There have been several attempts in recent years to portray the two sides as brothers in arms, with both the North and the South suffering equally.

Chapter 3

1. Alok K. Kanungo and Robert H. Brill, "Kopia, India's First Glassmaking Site: Dating and Chemical Analysis," *Journal of Glass Studies* Vol. 51 (2009): 11–25.

2. David Whitehouse, *Medieval Glass for Popes, Princes, and Peasants* (Corning, NY: Corning Museum of Glass, 2010).

3. Leeuwenhoek, to be sure, did not invent lenses. They were well known in antiquity and, much later, in Islamic science. See Dimitris Plantzos, "Crystals and Lenses in the Graeco-Roman World," *American Journal of Archaeology* 101, no. 3 (July 1996): 451–464. See also George Sines and Yannis A. Sakellarkis, "Lenses in Antiquity," *American Journal of Archaeology* 91, no. 2 (April 1987): 191–196; Vincent Ilardi, "Eyeglasses and Concave Lenses in Fifteenth-Century Florence and Milan: New Documents," *Renaissance Quarterly* 29, no. 3 (Autumn 1976): 341–360.

4. Quoted in Clifford Dobell, *Antony van Leeuwenhoek and His "Little Animals": Being Some Account of the Father of Protozoology & Bacteriology and His Multifarious Discoveries in these Disciplines* (New York: Russell & Russell, Inc., 1958), 41.

5. Dobell, *Antony van Leeuwenhoek*, 42.

6. Dobell, *Antony van Leeuwenhoek*, 117–118. All of Leeuwenhoek's fascinating correspondence has now been collected, edited, and translated into English in thirteen volumes, *Alle de brieven van Antoni van Leeuwenhoek/The Collected Letters of Antoni van Leeuwenhoek* (Amsterdam: Swets & Zeitlinger, Ltd., 1944–1988). Several of the original English translations of Leeuwenhoek's letters to the Royal Society are available at Jstor.org.

7. Dobell, *Antony van Leeuwenhoek*, 165–167.

8. For a discussion of the market for microscopes and lenses at the time of Leeuwenhoek, see Marc J. Ratcliff, *The Quest for the Invisible: Microscopy in the Enlightenment* (Farnham, UK: Ashgate, 2009).

9. It has long been accepted that only Europeans made major breakthroughs in lens technology. This is no longer a tenable position. Arab scientists of the ninth and tenth centuries made significant advances, both theoretical and practical. See Roshdi Rashid, "A Pioneer in Anaclastics: Ibn Sahl on Burning Mirrors and Lens," *Isis* 81, no. 3 (September 1994): 464–491.

10. Several popular books and articles have suggested that Vermeer's extremely accurate perspective was based on some sort of lens that projected the image he wanted onto a flat surface. A recent book tries to connect Vermeer and Leeuwenhoek, who were contemporaries and lived across the street from each other. There is at least the possibility of such a coventure but no hard evidence. Leeuwenhoek did not mention Vermeer in his correspondence, and no lenses were mentioned in the inventory produced on Vermeer's death. See Laura J. Snyder *Eye of the Beholder: Johannes Vermeer, Antoni van Leeuwenhoek and the Reinvention of Seeing* (New York: Norton, 2015).

11. Interview with Albert Noe, Columbus, Ohio, November 20, 1975, housed in The West Virginia and Regional History Center, Morgantown, WJ Call Number C208 R218.

12. For a broader view of glass history in the core areas of Appalachia, see Ken Fones-Wolf, *Glass Towns: Industry, Labor, and Political Economy in Appalachia, 1890–1930s* (Urbana: University of Illinois Press, 2007). For the widespread use of child labor, see James L. Flannery, *The Glass House Boys of Pittsburgh* (Pittsburgh: University of Pittsburgh Press, 2009).

13. Which is why, for example, single front windows in even the most expensive of American colonial houses generally required twelve panes of glass.

14. It is worth noting that Britain's success inspired successful production of plate glass in Belgium, Germany, and Russia, though never with the clarity or finish of French and English plate glass. Bohemia

(current-day Czechoslovakia) and Bavaria (current-day southern Germany, just west of Bohemia) continued to make and export large quantities of cheaper cylinder glass for residential and commercial windows.

15. Kenneth M. Wilson, "Plate Glass in America: A Brief History," *Journal of Glass Studies* Vol. 43 (2001): 145.

16. A 1941 review of technology in the glass field shows how much had changed and become automated between 1900 and 1940. See Charles John Phillips, *Glass: The Miracle Maker* (New York: Pitman Publishing Corporation, 1941).

17. Chimneys and bases of whale oil and, later, kerosene lamps were of glass. These lamps were a revolutionary form of lighting in the nineteenth century, allowing ordinary farmers and town dwellers to rise before dawn and stay up beyond sundown.

Chapter 4

1. Patrick Manning, *Migrations in World History* (New York: Routledge, 2005).

2. J. Thomas Barfield, *The Perilous Frontier* (London: Blackwell, 1989). See also Andrew Bell-Failkoff, *The Role of Migration in the History of the Eurasian Steppe: Sedentary Civilization vs "Barbarian" and Nomad* (New York: St Martin's Press, 2000).

3. Richard M. Eaton, *India in the Persianate Age: 1000–1765* (New York: Penguin, 2019).

4. Fred M. Donner, *The Early Islamic Conquests* (Princeton, NJ: Princeton University Press, 1981).

5. E. Matisoo-Smith and J. H. Robins, "Origins and Dispersal of Pacific Peoples: Evidence from mDNA Phylogenies of the Pacific Rat," *Proceedings of the National Academy of Sciences* 101, no. 24 (June 2004): 9167–9172. See also Janet M. Wilmshurst, Terry L. Hunt, C. Lipo, A. Anderson, and J. O'Connell , "High-Precision Radiocarbon Dating Shows Recent and Rapid Initial Human Colonization of East Polynesia," *Proceedings of the National Academy of Sciences* 108, no.5 (November 2010): 1815–1820.

6. Thomas D. Hall and P. Nick Kardullas, "Human Migration over Millennia: A World-System View of Human Migration, Past and Present," in *Mass Migration in the World-System: Past, Present, and Future*, ed. Terry-Ann Jones and Eric Mielants (Boulder, CO: Paradigm Publishers, 2010), 25.

7. José Ángel Navéjas, *Illegal: Reflections of an Undocumented Immigrant* (Urbana: University of Illinois Press, 2014), 3.

8. Emily Wang was kind enough to furnish me with a digital file of the original verbatim transcript of her interview with Zena. I am truly grateful to both Zena and Emily Wang for the opportunity to give a voice to an Arab Muslim immigrant woman. The pages of the digital file are not numbered. See Emily Wang, "Identity and Self-Reflection: Six Arab Immigrant Women Tell Their Stories," EdD dissertation, University of Michigan, 2017.

9. Kate Saller, *The Moon in Your Sky: An Immigrant's Journey Home* (Columbia: University of Missouri Press, 2014), 7–10.

10. Saller, *The Moon in Your Sky*, 33–34.

11. Saller, *The Moon in Your Sky*, 60–61.

12. Saller, *The Moon in Your Sky*, 77.

13. Saller, *The Moon in Your Sky*, 87–98.

14. An excellent comparative study of immigrants in two settings is Sandhya Shuka, *India Abroad: Diasporic Cultures of Postwar America and England* (Princeton, NJ: Princeton University Press, 2003).

15. I remember the lyrics of "Pastures of Plenty" from my folk-singing days and first heard it from Pete Seeger.

16. The literature on the Great Migration is vast. I have found particularly useful *Women, Gender, and Transnational Lives: Italian Workers of the World*, ed. Donna Gabaccia and Franca Lovetta (Toronto:

University of Toronto Press, 2002) and Melina L. de Jesús, ed., *Pinay Power: Theorizing the Filipina/American Experience* (New York: Routledge, 2005).

17. This discussion of the Great Migration relies on Kevin Brown, *Passage to the World: The Emigrant Experience 1807–1940* (Barnsley, UK: Seaforth Publishing, 2013).

18. Brown, *Passage.* 61.

19. Dirk Hoerder and Amarjit Kaur, eds., *Proletarian and Gendered Mass Migrations: A Global Perspective on Continuities and Discontinuities from the 19th to the 21st Centuries* (Leiden: Brill, 2013), 7.

20. José Ángel Navéjas, *Illegal : Reflections of an Undocumented Immigrant* (Urbana: University of Illinois Press, 2014), 14.

21. Navéjas , *Illegal,* 8.

22. Navéjas , *Illegal,* 23.

23. Saller, *Moon in Your Sky,*152–153.

24. Saller, *Moon in Your Sky,* 156.

25. Brown, *Passage to the World,* 71–75.

26. Aleksandr I. Solzhenitsyn, *The Gulag Archipelago, 1918–1956: An Experiment in Literary Investigation,* trans. Thomas P. Whitney (New York: Harper & Row, 1973), 4–5.

27. Steve A. Barnes, *Death and Redemption: The Gulag and the Shaping of Soviet Society* (Princeton, NJ: Princeton University Press, 2011), 11.

28. Barnes, *Death and Redemption,* 7–9.

29. *Global Compact for Safe, Orderly and Regular Migration,* https://refugeesmigrants.un.org/sites/default/files/180713_agreed_outcome_global_compact_for_migration.pdf.

30. *Global Compact,* paragraphs 9–1.

31. *Global Compact,* 13–14.

Chapter 5

1. Deuteronomy 20: 13–16

2. Quoted in E. G. Pulleybank, "The Origin and Nature of Chattel Slavery in China," *Journal of the Economic and Social History of the Orient* Vol. 1 Issue 2 (1958): 188. Here "corn" is the British term for wheat and millet, not maize, which was an American cereal.

3. Legal codes often attempted to define an impermeable boundary between slavery and nonslavery. They were rarely successful. The relations between slaves and nonslaves were too complicated.

4. Esteban Montejo, *The Autobiography of a Runaway Slave,* ed. Miguel Barnet, trans. Jocasta Innes (London: Bodley Head, Ltd., 1966).

5. Esteban, *Autobiography,* 7.

6. Esteban, *Autobiography,* 8.

7. Esteban, *Autobiography,* 18.

8. Esteban, *Autobiography,* 39.

9. Esteban, *Autobiography,* 22.

10. Esteban, *Autobiography,* 42.

11. See the writings of the "plantation school," such as Lloyd Best and Karl Polanyi Levitt, *Essays on the Theory of Plantation Economy: A Historical and Institutional Approach to Caribbean Economic Development* (Kingston, Jamaica: University of the West Indies Press, 2009).

12. A good introduction to writings of André Gunder Frank is *Theory and Methodology of World Development: The Writings of Andre Gunder Frank,* ed. Sing C. Chew and Pat Lauderdale (London: Palgrave Macmillan, 2010).

13. Eric R. Wolf and Sidney W. Mintz, "Haciendas and Plantations in Middle America and the Antilles," *Social and Economic Studies* 6, no. 3 (September 1957): 380–412.

14. Esteban, *Autobiography,* 24–25.

15. Arthur L. Stinchcombe, "Freedom and Oppression in the Eighteenth-Century Caribbean," in *Plantation Societies in the Era of European Expansion,* ed. Judy Bieber

(Aldershot, UK: Ashgate, 1997), 285–304. Many of the articles in this volume are useful for comparisons of slavery in the colonies of various nation-states. One sampling of nation-specific studies of slavery is Stuart B. Schwarz, *Slaves, Peasants, and Rebels: Reconsidering Brazilian Slavery* (Urbana: University of Illinois Press, 1992); Clive Y. Thomas, *Plantations, Peasants, and State: A Study of the Mode of Sugar Production in Guyana* (Los Angeles: University of California, Center for Afro-American Studies, 1984); see also Francisco A, Scarano, *Sugar and Slavery in Puerto Rico: The Plantation Economy of Ponce, 1800–1850* (Madison: University of Wisconsin Press, 1984).

16. Esteban, *Autobiography*, 26.

17. Esteban, *Autobiography*, 36.

18. Esteban, *Autobiography*, 40.

19. Esteban, *Autobiography*, 40.

20. Esteban, *Autobiography*, 29, 30, 32.

21. Esteban, *Autobiography*, 40.

22. Esteban, *Autobiography*, 45.

23. Esteban, *Autobiography*, 49.

24. See Sue Peabody, *"There Are No Slaves in France": The Political Culture of Race and Slavery in the Ancien Régime* (New York: Oxford University Press, 1996).

25. The classic cross-cultural comparison of slave rebellions is Eugene Genovese, *From Rebellion to Revolution: Afro-American Slave Revolts in the Making of the Modern World* (Baton Rouge: University of Louisiana Press, 1979). An article that connects slave rebellions to Native American resistance in the United States is Kelvin Santiago-Valles, "World-Historical Ties Among 'Spontaneous' Slave Rebellions in the Atlantic" *Review* (Fernand Braudel Center) 28, no. 1, The Black World and the World-System (2005): 51–83.

26. Esteban, *Autobiography*, 65–66.

27. Esteban, *Autobiography*, 69.

28. Esteban, *Autobiography*, 195.

29. Supplementary Convention on the Abolition of Slavery, the Slave Trade, and Institutions and Practices Similar to Slavery, 226 U.N.T.S. 3, entered into force April 30, 1957, Section One, Article One. http://www1.umn.edu/humanrts/instree/f3scas.htm.

30. The first scholar to write on modern slavery was Kevin Bales, *Disposable People: New Slavery in the World Economy* (Berkeley: University of California Press, 1999). See also Alexis A. Arnowitz, *Human Trafficking, Human Misery: The Global Trade in Human Beings* (Westport, CT: Prager, 2009).

31. Christien van den Anker, ed., *The Political Economy of New Slavery* (London: Palgrave Macmillan, 2004).

Chapter 6

1. Lynn Hunt, *Inventing Human Rights: A History* (New York: Norton, 2007), Introduction and Chapter 1, 15–68.

2. Attempts to shore up the historical basis for human rights generally take the form of selected documents supposedly showing the various waves of rights development. Typical of this genre is Samuel Moyn, *The Last Utopia: Human Rights in History* (Cambridge, MA: The Belnap Press of Harvard University Press, 2012). See also Lynn Hunt, *Inventing Human Rights* (New York: Norton, 2007). Recent research has shown that none of the earlier waves of assertion of rights was in fact headed directly toward what we think of as human rights today. There have certainly been earlier statements of rights, but they were always documents of their time, formulated within a local or sectarian context.

3. *United Nations Charter*, Preamble, Section 2.

4. *United Nations Charter*, Article 2, Section 7.

5. Quoted in Mary Ann Glendon, *A World Made New: Eleanor Roosevelt and the*

Universal Declaration of Human Rights (New York: Random House, 2001), 28.

6. Glendon, *A World Made New*, 30.

7. Alida Black, ed., *The Eleanor Roosevelt Papers: Vol. 1, The Human Rights Years, 1945–1948* (Detroit: Thomson Gale, 2001) 298.

8. Glendon, *A World Made New*, 31.

9. UN Assistant Secretary for Social Affairs Henri Laugier insisted on attending the first full meeting of the Human Rights Commission, though he was still recovering from being hit by a car and spoke from a wheelchair. One of his central concerns was petitions from people and groups claiming human-rights violations. Laugier reminded the members that they had no staff, no money to hold hearings, and no authority to collect evidence and investigate cases. In this situation Laugier suggested, "It is more important to acknowledge that this right is alive in the hearts and minds of men than merely to find it a dead-letter in an forgotten text." Black, *Roosevelt Papers*, 488.

10. Quoted in Glendon, *A World Made New*, 50.

11. Glendon, *A World Made New*, 50.

12. UNESCO, *Human Rights: A Symposium Prepared by UNESCO* (London: Allan Wingate, c. 1947), 11.

13. Quoted in Glendon, *A World Made New*, 146.

14. Illustrated in Glendon, *A World Made New*, 172.

15. Glendon, *A World Made New*, 189.

16. Black, *Roosevelt Papers*, 587.

17. Commission on Human Rights, Verbatim Record, Fourteenth Meeting (February, 4, 1947). Quoted in Black, *Roosevelt Papers*, 506.

18. Glendon, *A World Made New*, 141.

19. Some examples would include Maggie Lemere and Zoe West, eds., *Nowhere to be Home: Narratives from Survivors of Burma's Military Regime* (San Francisco: Voice of Witness, 2011; G.Thomas Burgess, *Race, Revolution and Human Rights in Zanzibar: The Memoirs of Ali Sultan Issa and Seif Sharif Hamad* (Athens: Ohio University Press, 2009); Lynn Stephen, ed. and trans., *Hear my Testimony: Maria Teresa Tula, Human Rights Activist of El Salvador* (Boston: South End Press, 1994); and Thomas C. Tirado, *Celsa's World: Conversations with a Mexican Peasant Woman* (Tempe: Arizona State University Center for Latin American Studies, 1991). Thoughtful discussions of this genre are Kay Schaffer and Siddonie Smith, *Human Rights and Narrated Lives: The Ethics of Recognition* (London: Palgrave Macmillan, 2004), and Gurminder K. Bhambra and Robbie Shillam, *Silencing Human Rights: Critical Engagements with a Contested Project* (London: Palgrave Macmillan, 2009).

20. See Sarah B. Snyder, *Human Rights Activism and the End of the Cold War: A Transnational History of the Helsinki Network* (Cambridge: Cambridge University Press, 2011).

21. Judith Blau and Alberto Moncada, *Human Rights: A Primer* (Boulder, CO: Paradigm Publishers, 2009), 15.

22. Judith Blau and Alberto Moncada, *Human Rights: Beyond the Liberal Vision* (Lanham, UK: Rowman & Littlefield, 2005).

23. See Michele Langfield, William Logan, and Mairead, Nic Craith eds., *Cultural Diversity, Heritage and Human Rights: Intersections in Theory and Practice* (London: Routledge, 2010). For a consideration of many human-rights issues today, see Gordon DiGiacomo, ed., *Human Rights: Current Issues and Controversies* (Toronto: University of Toronto Press, 2016).

24. The terrorist attacks of 9/11 did not stop the trend toward more and more assertions based on human rights. See Michael Goodhart and Anja Mihr, *Human Rights in the 21st Century: Continuity and Change Since 9/11* (London: Palgrave Macmillan, 2011).

Chapter 7

1. Tomé Pires, *The Suma Oriental of Tomé Pires*, trans. Armando Cortesao (London: Hakluyt Society, 1944), xxi–xxii.

2. See Christopher Bell, *Portugal and the Quest for the Indies* (London: Constable, 1974).

3. Pires, *Suma Oriental*, xxiii–xxiv.

4. Pires, *Suma Oriental*, 144.

5. Pires, *Suma Oriental*, 144. Although black pepper was indigenous only to the hills above the southwest coast of India (the current-day state of Kerala, India), long-distance trade, especially to China, encouraged pepper plantations in Southeast Asia well before the arrival of the Europeans. Mango cultivation also moved from India to island Souheast Asia by about 1000 CE.

6. Pires, *Suma Oriental*, xxxvi–xxxvii.

7. Karen Meier Reeds, *Botany in Medieval and Renaissance Universities* (New York: Garland, 1991). The author traces dramatic changes in the teaching of botany between 1500 and 1550. At the start of the sixteenth century the study of botany was limited to the investigation of medicinally useful herbs. Four decades later botany had widened to the general study of plants. In the earlier period students learned from books. By mid-century they were on field trips with their professors to examine local plants in the wild.,

8. Alan Titchmarsh, *Royal Gardners: The History of Britian's Royal Gardens* (London: BBC Books, 2004), 46. The botanical book that Turner wrote within a few decades of Tomé Pires's volme was titled *New Herball* (London: Collen, 2nd ed., 1568).

9. Two of the most famous early plant-hunters were John Tradescant and his son, who traveled in the first half of the 1600s. The father made it to Russia and brought back plants. He also received a variety of plants from the early British colonies in North America.

10. Jane Kilpatrick, *Fathers of Botany: The Discovery of Chinese Plants by European Missionaries* (London: Kew Publishing, 2014).

11. See Matteo Ricci, *China in the Sixteenth Century: The Journals of Matthew Ricci, 1583–1610*, trans. Louis J. Gallagher (New York: Random House, 1953).

12. The East India Company was a joint-stock trading company to which the English king had granted a monopoly of trade between India and England (later Great Britain). The EIC used British and locally recruited troops to conquer more and more land in India, often against the company's stated policy.

13. Corey Ross, Ecology and Power in the Age of Empire: Europe and the Transformation of the Tropical World (Oxford: Oxford University Press, 2017) 29.

14. Ross. *Ecology,* 29.

15. James Forbes Royale. *On the Culture and Commerce of Cotton in India and Elsewhere: With an Account of the Experiments Made by the Hon. East India Company up to the Present Time* (London: Smith, Elder and Co., 1851) 5-6.

16. Royale, *On the Culture,* 3.

17. Ross, *Ecology,* 9-30.

18. Royale, *On the Culture,* 44.

19. Royale, *On the Culture,* 241–243.

20. Royale, *On the Culture,* 247.

21. Gerald R. Tibbetts, *A Study of the Arabic Texts Concerning Material on Southeast Asia* (Leiden: Brill, 1979), 39.

22. Michael Flecker, "The Archaeological Excavation of the Tenth Century Intan Shipwreck," *British Archaeological Reports International Series* (Oxford: Archaeopress, 2002), 8.

23. Ross, *Ecology,* 140.

24. Ross, *Ecology,* 141.

25. Ross, *Ecology,* 142.

26. Ross, *Ecology,* 148.

Credits

Photo V2 3-2   HIP / Art Resource, NY

Photo V2 3-3   © Giancarlo Costa / Bridgeman Images

Photo V2 3-4   © Thomas Perrin, CNRS, UMR5608 Toulouse, FR" and citation of the original work

Photo V2 3-5   Universal History Archive/UIG / Bridgeman Images

Photo V2 3-6   From the collection of the author

Photo V2 3-7   Universal History Archive / Contributor

Photo V2 3-8   © New York Public Library / Stephen A. Schwarzman Building / Photography Collection, Miriam and Ira D. Wallach Division of Art, Prints and Photographs / Bridgeman Images

Photo V2 3-9   a9photo / Shutterstock

Photo V2 4-1   World History Archive / Alamy Stock Photo

Photo V2 4-2   © Giancarlo Costa / Bridgeman Images

Photo V2 4-3   Louis Le Breton / Wikipedia

Photo V2 4-4   Bettmann / Contributor

Photo V2 4-5   WhisperToMe / Wikipedia

Photo V2 4-6   Science History Images / Alamy Stock Photo

Photo V2 4-7   Shawshots / Alamy Stock Photo

Photo V2 4-8   Verhoeff, Bert / Anefo

Photo V2 4-9   Heritage Images / Contributor

Photo V2 5-1   Scala/Ministero per i Beni e le Attività culturali / Art Resource, NY

Photo V2 5-2   Look and Learn / Illustrated Papers Collection / Bridgeman Images

Photo V2 5-3   Estaben Montejo Mariano Pereira." MOAD Smithsonian Affiliate. Montejo, Estaben. *The Autobiography of a Runaway Slave.* Pantheon, January 1, 1849, Front Cover.

Photo V2 5-4   The Stapleton Collection / Bridgeman Images

Photo V2 5-5   © Archives Charmet / Bridgeman Images

Photo V2 5-6   Look and Learn / George Collection / Bridgeman Images

Photo V2 5-7   INTERFOTO / Alamy Stock Photo

Photo V2 5-8   Roger Arnold / Alamy Stock Photo

Photo V2 6-1   See Li / Alamy Stock Photo

Photo V2 6-2   Staatliche Kunstsammlungen Dresden / © Staatliche Kunstsammlungen Dresden / Bridgeman Images

Photo V2 6-3   RBM Vintage Images / Alamy Stock Photo

Photo V2 6-4   INTERFOTO / Alamy Stock Photo

Photo V2 6-5   Pearson Scott Foresman

Photo V2 6-6   Smith Archive / Alamy Stock Photo

Photo V2 6-7   Everett Collection Historical / Alamy Stock Photo

Photo V2 6-8   Keystone Press / Alamy Stock Photo

Photo V2 7-1   North Wind Picture Archives / Alamy Stock Photo

Photo V2 7-2   HIP / Art Resource, NY

Photo V2 7-3   UniversalImagesGroup / Contributor

Photo V2 7-4   © British Library Board / Robana / Art Resource, NY

Photo V2 7-5   Lithograph by G H Ford, reproduced in Ray Desmond

Photo V2 7-6   Victor Gillam

Photo V2 7-7   HIP / Art Resource, NY

Photo V2 7-8   Penrose, R. A. F. "The Tin Deposits of the Malay Peninsula
with Special Reference to Those of the Kinta District." The
Journal of Geology 11, no. 2 (1903): Plate II, Tin mine of Mr.
Foo Choo Choon, Tronoh, Perak, Malay peninsula. Accessed
July 1, 2021. http://www.jstor.org/stable/30054778.

Photo V2 7-9   Joerg Boethling / Alamy Stock Photo

Photo V2 7-10   Robert K. Chin / Alamy Stock Photo

Index